#MOMDAD

Dr. Candice Burney

DEDICATION

This book is dedicated to anyone who has had to face and overcome a stigma or stereotype. You are the reason I wrote this book. You are the voice that needs to be heard to change the false opinions and beliefs of society. You have no idea how powerful your story is. Help me to create the change that is needed by sharing your story. We can inspire people to be more open to different perspectives with less judgment and assumptions of others who are not like them.

CONTENTS

ACKNOWLEDGMENTS

I thank my daughters, Diamond and Destiny. You gave me the strength to challenge popular beliefs and pushed me to question rather than conform. My love for you got me through everything, and your love for me made it impossible to ever give up.

Thank you to my mom and dad for not being stereotypically perfect. I love the both of you for every ounce of who you are, and I am so grateful I wasn't raised in a bubble sheltered from the realities of life. Thank you for supporting this book and for being the best grandparents to Diamond and Destiny.

1 MY CONDITIONING

My earliest memories are from the time when I was about four to six years old and lived in Lakewood, California. Part of me was always athletic, what people in the eighties referred to as a tomboy. The other part of me loved dancing and singing every chance I had. My mother entered me in several beauty pageants where I sang and danced and memorized lines to win trophies that were twice my size. At one St. Patrick's Day pageant I won first place wearing a fluffy emerald-green pageant dress as I stood next to the award-winning trophy, which was six feet tall.

I was competitive and so were my parents. In Long Beach, where my father owned a vending business with my Grandpa Ken, it was not unusual in the eighties to see kids breakdancing on cardboard boxes on the street corners. One time, I wanted to breakdance to Michael Jackson's "Thriller" for the talent portion of the beauty pageant. So that I could practice, my dad offered some older kids a case of soda pop in exchange for a few breakdancing lessons for me, and they agreed. It was a hit at the pageant, and I had fun doing it.

At that age, I also auditioned for several commercials and TV shows with stars like Stevie Wonder, Peter Falk, and John Stamos. In fact, my mother told me John Stamos taught me how to tie my shoes, though I don't recall. My favorite audition was the one with Stevie Wonder. I believe it was an OshKosh commercial. When I auditioned, I was wearing my favorite overalls. He sat behind a white piano. He joked and sang with me, and at the end of the audition, he looked at me with his sunglasses on and told me to come back the next day and to tell my mom that he really liked my outfit. My mom was laughing when I told her, and I didn't know why until she shared with me that he was blind. He had completely fooled me, as I had no idea.

My best friend was African American and lived a few houses down from me. Her name was Rubystein

Angelika Tanika Newbill, but I just called her Tanika. She taught me all the hand-clapping routines, and we would put on shows for our parents. We had the whole hand clap and dance moves down to perfection, and we would perform them to anyone and everyone who was patient enough to watch us. They were so much fun! Tanika was the only friend I had at the time.

My parents had lots of friends. They would take me to parties all the time, and I would be the only child allowed there. They told me it was because I was well-behaved, but I just remember always sitting on the couch and people-watching. Back then there weren't cell phones or Nintendo Switches to play with. I was told to stay on the couch, and I would. Sometimes I would draw, but mostly I would sit there and observe. There would be people sniffing white lines of what looked like powdered sugar off little mirrors, and there was always lots of alcohol around. But things were different back then, and even though most of these people did drugs, they also had great careers, made good money, and they never mistreated me. If anything, they probably gave me more cake and ice cream than I needed, just to ensure I was happy on the couch.

One thing that hasn't changed is how expensive it

can be to live in Los Angeles County. My parents decided to buy a new home over an hour away in a small town called Moreno Valley, where it was less expensive. My dad planned to commute to work in Long Beach every day. We also had two dogs, Bubba, who was a white long-haired terrier, and Misty, who was a black-and-brown mix... but I was told we would only be able to take one of them with us. They left the decision up to me, and it was too hard to decide. So, I did what I thought was the most logical thing to do. I spun around with my eyes closed and my right arm out with a pointed finger and told my mom we would keep whichever dog I landed on. Bubba was the lucky winner. I was happy for Bubba but really sad for Misty. I was also sad that I had to say goodbye to Tanika.

Our home in Lakewood had thick orange shag carpet and wood paneling throughout. It was only a two-bedroom, so my older brother, Zach, and I shared a room that had a bunk bed. Our new home in Moreno Valley was a two-story home, with four bedrooms and three bathrooms and at least twice the size.

After we moved, my mom continued to take me to auditions, but it wasn't fun for me any longer. I would get car sick due to the long drive. About halfway to

Hollywood, every time, we would have to pull over on the side of the freeway because I would get sick. And the same would happen on the way back. By the time we got to the audition, I would already feel drained, and I didn't want to do it any longer. Just as I was getting ready to tell my mom I was over it, she told me that a major company had offered us $20,000 if I would be their spokesperson. As a six-year-old, I understood that was a lot of money, especially in 1986, and I could tell my mom really wanted me to do it. But she could also tell I didn't want to, and she knew how car sick I was getting each time and that we would have to drive even more if we accepted that commitment, so we declined. And that was the end of the auditions and the pageants. What the pageants and auditions taught me as a child was how to be sociable and how to memorize well (which came in handy later), and it gave me confidence. The experience I had with the breakdancers on the street was just as meaningful as the experiences I had with the superstars we would see on TV, which also taught me we can learn from anyone.

I also left behind my first track team in Lakewood. I had only run one race with them before we moved. It was the 100-meter dash and I was wearing a black-and-white Wildcats uniform. I remember standing nervously at the starting line waiting for the horn to blow as I quickly scanned my competition. As the horn sounded, I took off as fast as I could. I was in the lead the entire time and I was almost at the finish line when I decided to look back. That fear of seeing if anyone was close to me allowed someone to pass me, and I ended up in second place. At the time, I didn't realize it was a life lesson, but it was. In that brief moment when I looked back, it slowed me down. I didn't lose the race because I was incapable of winning. I lost the race because I broke focus and got in my own way worrying about everyone else. I continued to get in my own way throughout much of my life, and I still do at times, but I try to remember that moment and how it taught me to focus on the things I can control.

A few days after we moved into our new home, I met Tara. She lived across the street; we were the same age, and her older brother was the same age as my brother. I liked going to their house because her mom was always making goodies, like those Chex Mix muddy buddies and the sugar cookies with the Hershey's chocolate Kiss in the middle. The area where we lived was still up and coming so we took the bus across town to the closest elementary school. Tara and I hung out together at school. At home, we would make up dance routines, play with Barbies, and play around outside. Although I still missed Tanika, it was nice to have made a friend so quickly.

My family nickname was Buns. I had been born with a little bubble butt and was surprised by the attention it would cause. A boy in my second-grade class kept asking me if he could touch it, and I continuously told him no. I told the teacher and she told him to stop but then she would get busy again and stop paying attention. As a group of us were working on an assignment, the boy crawled under the desk. I was wearing a dress that day, and he reached under my dress and touched my private part. I kicked him and felt violated. I ran and told the teacher; she just told him to stop again, but that was it. That night, I told my parents, and my dad told me I had his permission to beat someone's ass if they touched me. So the following week, I was drinking water out of the water fountain during recess when that same boy ran by and grabbed my butt. I decided to run after him. When I caught up to him, he turned around, and I kicked him as hard as I could between the legs.

I ended up in the principal's office, but he didn't mess with me after that. If my dad hadn't given me the confidence to defend myself, I don't know if I would have. I would have been afraid to get in trouble at school. It felt good to know my parents trusted that if I did something like that at school, it was to protect myself, and I didn't need to be scared of getting in trouble with both the school and my parents should I be placed in that situation. I share this story because it was the first time I was touched in that way, and it happened at school, in the middle of the day, after this young boy had been told to stop by the teacher. It is also my first memory of my "asset" attracting the wrong type of attention from boys. In the end, I was happy to leave that school. I started third grade at a newer school closer to our home.

I liked the new school, and I met more friends, including Shannon, who lived up the street from us in a new housing development that was connected to our subdivision. Shannon had two brothers and a sister. She shared a room with her sister, but I would stay over sometimes when her sister stayed out. Her house was always really clean, with clear runners laid out strategically on the heavy walk areas. We would wipe our feet with Lysol on a rag before entering the home, which when I became a parent, I thought was brilliant of her mom, with all the fun smells that come with teenagers. It always smelled good in their house, and they had perfect triangle vacuum marks throughout the carpet. I would feel bad at times because my hair smelled like cigarette smoke from my house, and so I would always be sure to shower and wash my hair before going to bed in one of their beds. Shannon and I liked to watch MTV, make our own outside adventures, and prank call people. One night we tried my mom's vodka in the cabinet and replaced what we drank with water and put it back. We were good at creating fun together.

On days when I didn't have school, I sometimes went to work with my dad. Every morning, if I wasn't going to work with him, he would come into my room between three and four o'clock in the morning to kiss me and say goodbye, and then I would fall back to sleep. If I was going to work with him, he would wake me up a little earlier so I could get ready. He wasn't much of a talker, so we would listen to talk radio during the commute and just enjoy the drive. We would arrive at his warehouse first, to transfer from his truck to the work van, and say hi to my Grandpa Ken (when he would get to the warehouse before us). Then we would head off to the different accounts to service the vending machines, snack machines, and arcade games. He would be impressed by the cases of soda pop I could carry, and he allowed me to fill up the machines even though I was much slower at it than he was.

Sometimes when I went to work with him, I would hang out with Grandpa Ken instead. I would play at the warehouse, climb on the high stacked piles of soda pop cases, and ride on the yellow pallet jack as if it were a scooter. The three of us would go to the pancake house and eat breakfast, and they would talk business while I listened and observed. Grandpa enjoyed teaching me about business, and he had a sense of humor. He would joke about things like how he would feed me to the sharks if I didn't listen. One day he drove me to the garment district in LA. He told me I could spend $100 on merchandise I thought I could re-sell. I would have to pay him the $100 back, but I could keep whatever I had leftover as a profit. I bought a few ring watches, some mood rings, and little eyeshadow makeup kits that were shaped like a butterfly. I then went to school and sold the items out of my backpack to the kids who had money. I was able to pay my grandpa back, and I made a profit of $40. I felt rich. Both Dad and Grandpa were good at teaching me about money and its value. They would explain to me when they would pull $200 out of one vending machine that the $200 was not the profit. The machine needed to be filled back up again with soda pop and snacks. The difference, minus our time, would be the profit.

When school started back, I was entering the fifth grade, and I ran for student body vice president. My mom, who was extremely clever, helped me win with a speech that rhymed, and everyone loved it. I don't remember all of it, but I know it ended with "So vote for me, your new VP, and have a truly awesome year!" I enjoyed participating in school and at assemblies. I would act in school plays, with my early favorite being Shakespeare's *The Taming of the Shrew*. However, my most vivid memory of fifth grade is from the end of the school year, when I was supposed to make a speech. I was also being presented with Student of the Month, which my mom knew but I didn't. Unfortunately, I got the chickenpox, but my mom didn't want me to miss out on my award or on giving my speech, so she covered my entire body in pink calamine lotion. I was also wearing a fluffy light-pink dress, and while I felt ridiculous, I went on stage to make my speech.

I don't think many people noticed the pink lotion plastered all over me, which made me happy, as I didn't want to draw too much attention to myself. But just as I completed my speech, I noticed my mother running up the middle aisle with a gigantic balloon that said BUNS on it! A big ass balloon with the letters B-U-N-S. No one knew that was my nickname in my family, so imagine the confusion and the questions I received after. Many people didn't let that one go for a while, and I can't say I blame them. It may not have been funny to me that day, but I found humor in it eventually.

I also met my friend Susan in elementary school. She didn't live within walking distance as Tara and Shannon did, but we would often hang out. I remember she had the coziest bed, and I loved her family. Susan was fearless and just did what she wanted to do; I loved that about her. One night we "borrowed" my mom's convertible Mustang while she was sleeping and drove all around town feeling super cool. I don't know how we didn't get caught. We also wrote songs together, and we would have deep life conversations. We had separate sets of friends at times, but our spirits always gravitated to each other and she always just felt like family.

While speeches and student body stuff were fun, I was missing the adrenaline I had felt when I raced and competed. I wanted that feeling back. It wasn't until middle school that I got back into sports. I made the track team, cross-country team, and basketball team. I also joined a dojo outside of school, where I practiced karate and kickboxing. Our basketball team went undefeated through our eighth-grade year, and my track and cross-country coach helped me realize a deeper physical strength I didn't know I had. He was dedicated and knowledgeable and pushed everyone hard. I grew so much athletically from him, and I think anyone he coached would say the same. He was often made fun of for wearing short shorts and called a pervert for some of the comments he would make to the girls, though from my personal experience, that was only encouraging the girls to get sports bras. After having coached as an adult myself, I admire all he put into making us better athletes and showing us our potential. I realized the lasting impact a coach can make on a young athlete.

May you rest in peace, Coach.

Freshman Year

By the time I entered high school I felt prepared for it, sort of. I started puberty late and thankfully when I did, my dad was home. I remember not being sure what to do. I yelled for my dad, who was downstairs; he wasn't sure what to do either, so I sat on the toilet for over an hour while he went to the store and bought everything under the sun. Then he gently tossed the bag into the bathroom and I eventually figured it out.

I wanted to do anything and everything to make the most of my high school experience. I just didn't want to do it in four years. I wanted to do it in three. In the second week of my freshman year, I walked into the counseling office and asked the counselor to write me a three-year plan instead of a four-year plan. The counselor was kind and went over all the pros and cons of the decision I was making and made it very clear it would not be easy but said that if I stuck to the plan it was possible. The plan consisted of me going to zero period (offered before school) and completing the Regional Occupational Program (ROP) to earn credits by working for free somewhere, which I could do after practice and on weekends. Additionally, I was on the volleyball, basketball, cross-country, and track teams and still found time outside of school for kickboxing on Saturdays.

In high school, most people's perception of me was that my homelife was pretty good. People thought we had good money, because my mom had a red convertible Mustang and I lived in a two-story home with a pool. And I always had the best candy at my house from my dad's vending business—you know, the full-size candy bars, Famous Amos cookies, and a variety of chips you could choose from, all in a box above the fridge.

My father was a functional alcoholic, but you could hardly tell. He worked fourteen-hour days, and he worked his ass off. He only took Sundays off, and every Sunday morning he would go grab donuts, and I would wake up to a dozen donuts and the funny papers (the comics section of the newspaper). He simply liked to spend his evenings with his best friend "Bud"—short for Budweiser. My mother was full of energy; there was never a dull moment with her. She could be intense to be around at times but was also the one person you would want in your corner should anything go wrong. My friends loved being around her, and she loved to entertain. I'm sure my parents had been happy at some point in their marriage, but at this stage, it was mostly arguing. Two wonderful imperfect people screaming at each other nightly over anything and everything. They began living separate lives but still in the same house.

They were trying to do what they felt was right and wanted to stay married for my brother and me, but my brother and I were over it. It got so bad that toward the end of their marriage, my dad built a wall separating part of the home; my mother lived downstairs, and my father lived upstairs, while they both shared the kitchen. Some of my parents' arguments would just be some harsh name-calling. Other times things would get broken, and then I would help clean up.

My parents got married when my brother, Zach, was two. He was my father's son from a previous relationship, and marrying my mom helped my father gain custody of him. I came into the world when my brother was four. Zach decided he wanted to live with his biological mother in Oregon when I was twelve. The only good part about that for me was that I got to move into the big bedroom; other than that, I was extremely sad. He had lived with us all my life, and now when my parents would argue, I didn't have him to joke about it with or even to fight with and play video games with.

It was the first time I ever saw my dad cry. I think it

hit my mom hard, too, but neither of them ever really talked about it, at least not to me. I never blamed my brother, nor would I ever. I don't know if my parents blamed each other or not, but it felt like they resented each other for many reasons. My mom started dancing on a country line-dancing team that she created as an outlet. My dad started staying the night in Long Beach more and more, and the dynamics were off.

I used sports as my outlet, and I sang in the choir. I loved singing Mariah Carey and Whitney Houston (or trying to, at least). When I tried out for show choir, I auditioned with Mariah Carey's version of "Open Arms," a cappella. I must not have butchered it too badly, because I made the team, and it was a memorable experience. There were many talented singers in our choir, four of whom went on to become professional singers, some on television, some as background singers for popular artists, and others with their own business teaching singing lessons. Our choir teacher had gone to school with Snoop Dogg, and I always thought she was the coolest for that.

I also loved dancing. At one point I was certain I would become a choreographer like Paula Abdul, and the fact that she had been a cheerleader for the Lakers made her even more of an idol to me. I lived in my own little world a lot, in my room with the door closed, writing poems and songs and hitting stop on the tape deck, rewinding, relistening, and making sure I knew all the words to all the songs I liked.

I felt I was good at all the sports I played, but not a superstar in any of them. I made the basketball team because I was fast and I had good anticipation, so I could steal the ball easily, but then just as quickly as I would steal it, I would either miss the fast-break lay-up or dribble the ball off my foot. My coach told me I made the team because I had heart, not because I could play. Though I did make some baskets here and there and was far better at jump shots. I loved basketball, and I was a hard-core Lakers fan. I knew fundamentally more about basketball than any other sport, but my best sport at that time was track and field. Our coach always had me competing in four events (which was the most we could compete in). I also competed on a club track team outside of school, where I made it to the Junior Olympics and placed third in the javelin throw in Atlanta. I never broke any records, but I was a reliable option for my coaches.

I initially started playing volleyball just to keep in

shape between track and basketball, but I found it was so much fun. While I was on the shorter end at five foot, five inches, I had hops and had become an outside hitter. I wouldn't learn the fundamentals of volleyball until much later in my life, but I had already realized how important sports were to me. Whether I was stealing a basketball, running my ass off, spiking a volleyball, or sparring in kickboxing, the process of getting to the point where I could compete, taught me discipline, respect, perseverance, and how to be part of a team. It also taught me how important it is to prepare and practice… no matter what it is.

In high school, I had just as many guy friends as girlfriends. I completely trusted the guy friends I had, as I often felt like one of them. One day a track teammate of mine asked if I wanted to ditch school for a couple of periods and play this new video game that had come out. It was a Friday, and I didn't have much going on in my next two classes, plus I missed playing video games with my brother, so I agreed. There was a ditch behind the school, and we walked that way to his house. We were just joking and laughing about random things all the way there.

When we got to his house, no one was home. We

went up to his room, and I sat on the edge of his bed right in front of the television and asked what the new game was that he got. Instead of answering my question, he pushed me on my back, aggressively pulled down my pants, and told me we weren't really there to play video games. I was initially paralyzed from being shocked and confused. I hadn't ever felt any romantic tension between us. I didn't see him in that way at all. He got on top of me; he was heavy, really heavy. He played football and had more of a big, broad-football physique. On the track team, he only competed in shot put. I was still a virgin and I still had my underwear on, but he was trying to have sex with me as I fought to get out from underneath him. I was able to keep my underwear on, but he was still able to make me bleed. My adrenaline kicked in and I got out from under him, grabbed my pants, and ran. I ran down his stairs, out his front door (still with my pants in my hand), past a neighbor of his who was outside and definitely saw me, but I kept running until I got back to the ditch. Then I put my pants back on and continued to run all the way back to the school. Luckily, I got back right before practice, so I went straight to the gym and changed into my track gear.

I didn't see him until the next day at practice. I

approached him and I was pissed. I told him that I had thought he was my friend, and that I couldn't believe he'd tried to have sex with me when I clearly didn't want to. He answered that he was sorry and had thought I would be cool with it. We didn't stay friends, and I decided not to tell anyone. I thought I would be judged for ditching and just not believed since he was popular and well-liked. After that experience, I would second-guess all the guy friends I had and try to assess whether they really were my friends or not. It sucked. Looking back, I wish I had said something, because had I not been strong enough, I do feel he would have raped me. And while I wasn't yelling, "No," not for one second in that situation had I consented.

Typically, during lunchtime, I would walk around, and hang out with different groups of friends, rather than the same one every day. I felt like I was a little popular. I didn't have the status of a prom queen or king... It was more that, because I was active and involved in so many activities that I knew a lot of people and they knew me. While I'd had crushes on boys in elementary school and middle school, I had not had a serious boyfriend.

About halfway through my freshman year, there was this guy who started following me around. He would wait outside my classes, look at me, and wave through the little square window in the door during class and constantly ask me out. I would politely decline each time. He didn't scare me or make me feel uncomfortable; he was more of a nuisance. I didn't recognize him, and he didn't play on any of the sports teams. I wouldn't see him around campus (unless he was following me), and he was a grade or two higher than me. None of my friends knew who he was, and the few people who did know of him just said that he ditched a lot and they never really saw him in class (possibly because he was always standing outside of mine).

The Dare

One day at lunch I was sitting with one of my friends and telling her about the guy who kept asking me out. I told her that I kept kindly refusing but wasn't sure how to make him stop.

And then came *the dare*; this is the moment when it all started.

She dared me to go out with him and then break up with him in two weeks. That way, I could say we had "tried" and it hadn't worked, and that would be that. I felt that was a great idea… and besides, I was too competitive to turn down a dare. Later that day after choir practice when he was waiting outside of my class, I simply said, "OK, we can go out." I didn't know how all that worked, and I certainly didn't realize how seriously he would take it.

The two weeks passed, and then it was Valentine's Day. I couldn't bring myself to break up with him on that day. I had only seen him a few times (all during school) in those two weeks, but I was too nice for that. So I waited. Then it was his birthday in March, so that wasn't good timing either. As I spent more time with him, he started to open up about his life. His issues made mine seem silly, and to be honest, it was a nice distraction. If I could focus on his issues and try to help, my issues just didn't seem that bad. He had two older brothers who were in and out of prison for gang-related murders, and his father had committed suicide when he was just six months old. He loved his mother, who was mixed-race with Japanese and African American heritage. He would often express how he wanted to do something great with his life to take care of her and help his brothers when they got out.

People started to realize we were dating. I was a White girl with blue-green eyes and light-brown hair, and he was African American, with darker skin and long braids. He wanted to be a famous rapper. He would write raps about me and record them and constantly remind me that I was the most beautiful thing on the planet. He would come to my games, and meets, where he would watch from a distance and tell me I did great, even if I knew I had sucked that day. We would get racist remarks when out in public, and it would only bother him when it was directed toward me. I felt loved and cared for.

I was afraid to tell my parents I had a boyfriend. It's just an uncomfortable conversation, but I told them, and my mom was able to meet him but was not too thrilled about him. It wasn't his race with her; it was more his demeanor, and she didn't want me to see him. So I did the logical thing… I started sneaking out, sneaking him in, skipping classes… in a young love-ish way. But I was still on top of my schedule. I was sure to never skip any classes on game days and never miss a test.

One night my mother cooked some steak. I loved it when she cooked. That night I snuck him in through my bedroom window, which was on the second floor. He had to walk or bike several miles, climb the side yard fence, hop on the tile roof, then get to my window. We were watching television, and I shared my plate with him, then decided to go get more food.

Call it a mother's intuition. She put more on my plate but gave me a look as if to say, "You better not." I went back upstairs while silently reeling off about fifty prayers in the hope that I had read that interaction wrong. I got back to the room and closed the door, but the next thing I heard was the frightening sound of stomps coming up the stairs. It happened so quickly, there was no time to react. The door flung open, and she caught him mid-chew. She screamed at him to get out, grounded me, and took away the car keys I had just been given.

Being young and foolish, and perhaps overreacting a bit… I decided to run away.

I didn't have a plan, but it was now summer, so I wasn't missing any school. My boyfriend's brother's girlfriend invited me to stay with her in West Hollywood. She said she was a traveling masseuse but didn't have a car. She said she would pay me $50 for each appointment she had, and all I had to do was be her driver. That sounded like a great deal. So, I took her up on that offer, snuck my keys back, and drove to West Hollywood. I slept on the floor and took her to about four appointments a day. In my mind, I was making good money. I stayed there for two weeks. During those two weeks, I would call different friends asking them to call my parents and tell them I was OK. I ended up coming back home because my mother told me she was going to put my dog to sleep. I doubt she would have done that, but the threat worked. I was starting to miss home anyway. When I got back, my mother told me that she had spoken with her mother, my Grandma Hazel, and was sending me to Florida to live with her.

Off I went to start my sophomore year in Winter Park, Florida, with Grandma Hazel. Most of my family on my mother's side lived in Florida and being back around them made me happy. I had the greatest times with my cousins. I moved into my Grandpa Floyd's old room, which held many emotions for me. The last time I had seen him alive, he had given me $50 and told me to put it toward a nice dress one day. I put it in an envelope and put it in a safe, where it still sits. He wasn't the giving type, you might say, and I knew his giving that to me was a big deal… so I just kept it. My mother told me he had been harsh to his kids as a military father, and I don't know if he ever regretted any of his actions or not, but I have memories of him dressed as Santa, taking my cousins and me for a ride in a trailer connected to a tractor over the holidays, and telling me stories about his time in the military in Korea and the pretty ladies out there. In my pre-teen years, he would flip me off, call me #1, and ask me to grab him a cup of ice and a Pepsi. He also referred to my breasts as camel humps. It was just his sense of humor. Hearing about the cruel side of him just gave me hope that maybe people can change.

One day while he and I were sitting on the porch, we saw a black bird playing with a white bird. He commented that they shouldn't be playing together and that they should be playing with their own kind. I challenged his opinion and said it looked like they were playing with each other because they liked each other. Perhaps they came from the same place. He didn't comment back. He didn't say anything at all. I still sometimes wonder what he was thinking at that moment. I'm sure it was a smart-ass remark, but in serious moments, we had a silent mutual respect for each other. I think his silence at that moment was him respecting my opinion, knowing that his was different.

My Grandma Hazel was amazing. Every morning I would wake up to either corned beef and hash or Jimmy Dean sausage and eggs. I would sneak late-night calls back home to my boyfriend, but she never knew, and I would have never disrespected her if she had caught me.

The high school I was going to was brand new and looked like a college. I tried out for and made the basketball team. A few games in, my grandmother invited the entire basketball team over for her infamous vegetable soup with fried cornbread. Now, vegetable soup may not be a favorite meal for most teenagers, but any teenager who ate my grandmother's version was sure to be a fan right after. Anything she cooked was great.

It was coming up to Christmas break in Florida, and I was flying back home to see my mom and dad for two weeks. During those two weeks, I saw my friends and, of course, my boyfriend. The day I was supposed to return to Florida, I got on the plane, but then I got off. I watched it take off and just sat there for a minute and cried. I loved my family in Florida, and my grandmother was easy to live with, but it just felt like I was missing something. All the friends I had grown up with were in California. And perhaps running away had been a terrible thing to do... but I wasn't a bad kid. Despite all of this, I was still on track to graduate early, still played sports, and never did drugs or anything like that. I just wanted to be home. After sitting at the airport for a couple of hours, I ended up taking a taxi home. I figured there would be anger, so I mentally prepared myself as I walked up the driveway. My mother was indeed pissed that I'd gotten off the plane. After a lengthy conversation and many apologies, I was allowed to stay home in California.

Junior Year

To finish my sophomore year, I had to attend a different school temporarily, due to availability. This school was closer to where my boyfriend lived, and more people knew him there. At my previous school, no one had cared that we were dating, but at this school, it appeared to be a problem. No one liked the fact that I was dating him, mostly because I was White, and this was made very clear. In my second week, a group of girls approached me wanting to confirm who I was dating. They then told me to stop dating him and to stick with my own race. Interracial dating was common when I was in high school, so I just told them to stop worrying about me and walked away. Then, the following week, I was on the way to leave campus after school and had to walk past a row of portables. There were usually lots of people walking through there, but there were only a few on this day. I had this eerie feeling in the pit of my stomach, because something felt off. Sure enough, right as I was about to turn around and go back, a paperback book was thrown right at the back of my head, then another and another… and then the punches and the kicks came. During this ass-beating, I was getting called several derogatory names; "White trash," "hoe," "slut," "wigger," "Stop trying to be Black," they told me, and I was warned and should have listened. If I hadn't learned defensive skills in karate and kickboxing, I felt it would have been worse. Far worse. Due to the number of people kicking, slapping, and punching me, I just held my own the best I could and protected my ears and face and kept my stomach tight as I lay on the asphalt in a balled-up position. Eventually, a campus yard duty blew her whistle loudly, and everyone scattered.

When I got to the house, my dad was home. He looked me up and down and noticed the scratches all over my arms, along with some blood. He could tell I had been in a fight. He simply asked if I was OK and if I had started it. I told him I got my ass beat because I had a Black boyfriend. He told me that next time if I didn't beat their ass, he would beat mine… and then asked if I was hungry.

I appreciated that about my dad. He never overreacted to things. He just stayed calm and did his best to understand what I was going through. I'm sure he knew I would've preferred not to get jumped that day. As a parent now, I realize how difficult that was to do and how much self-control that took.

When questioned by the school the next day I lied and said I hadn't recognized any of the guys or girls who had jumped me. What good would that have done? Coincidentally, a spot opened up back at Canyon Springs High School, where I had started at, and I would be able to transfer back the following week. During the remainder of that week, I was on high alert, but nothing else happened. Perhaps I gained respect for not being a snitch? I have no idea.

So much happened that summer after my sophomore year. My relationship changed. I found out that the little boy who was always at my boyfriend's house, who I had been told was his nephew, was actually his son... yes, son! Did I leave the relationship at that point? No, of course not. I was sixteen and bought the story that he was telling me the truth because he loved me and wanted to be with me. It all made complete sense to my young, naïve mind. He had also dropped out of high school and said it was for his rapping career so he could take care of me. Well, that sounded fantastic.

My parents were still trying their best to hang on to their marriage, but it just kept getting worse. By this point, they were awkward roommates at best. I just wanted to hurry up and graduate so they could move on with their lives. They were both stressed and hanging on by a thin thread for me. I just wanted to help give them peace.

My mother kept us on our toes. She had been raised in rough, poor circumstances, with four brothers and two sisters in a three-bedroom home. She would tell me stories of Grandpa Floyd beating all of them for no reason, or because he felt one of them was guilty of something but didn't know which one. She had done her best to recondition herself once she was out of the house and living her own life. Her ways of teaching us lessons often had good intentions but poor delivery.

One morning she was getting ready to take me to school, and when we got in the car, I grabbed the last piece of gum from the middle console as she was backing up from the driveway… She stopped the car. I looked at her in confusion and saw she was looking at me in anger. She pretended she hadn't just seen me grab the last piece of gum and asked if I could give her a piece. Knowing that I had just taken it and it was in my mouth I guiltily told her I had taken the last piece. She went on and on about how she really wanted a piece of gum and made me feel like shit over it. I know she intended to say, "Hey, honey, I realize you just took the last piece of gum, but when you do that in the future, it is polite to ask if someone else wants it or if they would like to share it with you." Instead, I went to school feeling like an asshole and ended up feeling bad that my mom didn't get a piece of gum that day because of me. But I got the message.

Another time, when I was little, I was upset about something at the grocery store and started throwing a fit. So she threw herself on the floor and began kicking and screaming and throwing her own fit. While I admit I definitely stopped and was then focused on getting her to stop and get up, it was not something you see every day. My mother is truly one of a kind in that regard. Perhaps her methods were not popular, but they could be effective, nonetheless.

I began my junior year, which was also my senior year, since I was still on track with the plan. I checked in with the counselor and found I had to double up on a few classes. My schedule was tough, but I was determined. The job I was working at for school credit, Champs, ended up hiring me as a paid employee as soon as I completed the school program. In school, my life felt good. I was progressing, playing varsity sports, and on track to graduate a year early. My personal life was a different story.

My parents' marriage continued to get worse, as did my relationship. I would lie to my parents to make him look good, so much so that I would believe it myself. I didn't want to be wrong about him. I felt I had already risked a lot to support him and make it work, so I did my best to make that thought into a reality.

Prom was coming up, and I really wanted to go, especially since it would be my only opportunity. It was being held in Palm Springs. I knew my boyfriend didn't have any money and wouldn't be able to buy the prom tickets, but I lied to my parents and said he had. I figured we would just hang out for the night and I would pretend I had gone to prom. I would have bought us tickets, but I didn't have the money either, and I didn't want to ask my parents because it would have made my boyfriend look bad. They agreed to let me go since the tickets had already been purchased, and to top it off, my mom surprised us with a limo to take us on the hour-long drive to Palm Springs! So I helped him rent a tux with all the money I had, and my mom and dad helped me with the dress. It was a beautiful pearl-white silk dress. We took pictures in the front yard near the brick patio and rose plants, then hopped in the limo and went all the way to Palm Springs.

Prom was being held at a golf course, but since we didn't have tickets to get inside, we had to figure out something to do until it was over. My mother had instructed the driver to take us there and back, so driving around in the limo wasn't an option. We walked around the golf course, took two lounge chairs off of someone's patio, hung out at the top of a hill, and looked at the stars. Then, all of a sudden, the sprinklers came on! My soft, silky dress quickly became a see-through, soggy mess, and I had to take my heels off as we sprinted back down the hill. We waited outside the prom building doors as we listened to the music playing inside… and I just imagined that we had been able to go in. I pictured myself dancing and everyone loving my dress. In my head, it was a beautiful night. On the way home, I had just enough for Taco Bell, and then we called it a night.

Meanwhile, I decided to try the Hollywood thing out again. This time, modeling instead of pageants and acting. My mother went with me to a swimsuit photo shoot. During the shoot, I was approached and asked if I would consider doing Playboy. We were invited to the Playboy mansion and told it would pay well. I had just turned seventeen and I didn't want my "asset" to be shared with the world in that way, so I declined. My mother was completely on board with my decision, but we were both incredibly flattered by the invitation. Another opportunity came about from my martial arts experience and I was invited to audition to be one of the Power Rangers in the coming months, and I was excited about that opportunity.

As it got closer to graduation, I had mixed feelings. I was happy I'd stuck to the plan and was graduating a year early, but my close friends were all graduating the following year, and I would have loved another chance at the prom thing.

College

Immediately following my graduation, my parents filed for divorce. My mother ended up falling in love with her friend's ex-husband, who lived in Northern California. She then transferred with her job to Sacramento to secure them a place to live. My father was often staying in Long Beach at his warehouse, but he was good about ensuring I had food and money to get me through the week and for stuff I needed. For a while, I had a four-bedroom, two-bath, two-story house with a pool all to myself at the age of seventeen. That wasn't terrible. In fact, I decided to have a handful of friends over one day.

We were all swimming and playing games. A few of them brought a couple of people I didn't know, but I trusted who they were with. That was, until I noticed my dad's bedroom door was open. His room was off-limits, and I had made that known. There was no reason for anyone to go in there. My heart dropped, because in his desk drawer was where he would leave my money for the week. I immediately went to the desk to check, and it was gone. Then I frantically went to my room, where I kept my jewelry, and noticed my tennis bracelet was gone. It was the only thing my dad had ever gone out and bought me (he would typically give cash instead), and it meant a lot to me. Then I noticed games were missing, and people were sitting there playing them, so someone had to have seen something. I was angry. Here they were in my house, swimming in my pool, eating our good snacks, and I had trusted them… yet they were stealing from me right in front of my face!

I told everyone that I was going to take a shower and that when I got out, I wanted everything back that had been taken from me. If not, I wanted everyone out of the house. I left one of my girlfriends in charge of getting my stuff. When I was done, I had my games back and about half of the money. The rest of the money and the bracelet were still missing. So I told everyone to get out. I never found out who did it, nor did I ever have another party at my house.

When my dad did stay at the house, he would sometimes pick me up from work. My car had been sold as part of the divorce. One unforgettable day, he picked me up from work, and I just started crying. He just looked at me as he often did, with a calm yet concerned expression, and asked me, "Are you pregnant?" My dad and I had this thing where we just couldn't lie to each other. I remember one year, I was eight years old and he was doing tile work in the house, and I asked him if Santa Claus was real, and he just looked at me and said, "No." So I followed up with questions about the Easter Bunny and the Tooth Fairy, and he continued to be straight with me. As a mom, I completely understood why my mom was upset about it, but at the same time, I appreciated the honesty. So when he asked me if I was pregnant, I was honest and admitted that I was.

I called and told my mom, and understandably, she

wasn't happy. Nor would I be auditioning for the Power Ranger role. Not wanting to leave my boyfriend I turned down the partial athletic scholarship I had been offered to Kansas State and decided to stay local and go to junior college instead. The college I wanted to go to was Long Beach State. It had a cool gymnasium in the shape of a pyramid, and I just wanted to play in it one day. I had always loved competing in the track meets we had there on my travel track team, and I had often envisioned myself going to school there.

Education was important to me. Smart as they all are, no one in my immediate family had graduated from college yet. My Grandpa Ken had dropped out of school in the third grade to help support his family by selling oranges and razor blades, two for a nickel. His grind ended up motivating him to start the vending business years later. While my Grandpa Ken nor my father had earned a degree, they taught me about business, street smarts, and common sense… which in my opinion was invaluable. My mother had some college experience but had found a career in the railroad industry that would provide her with a good retirement without having to earn a degree.

Graduating from college was a goal I wanted to

achieve for myself. I didn't have a car, so I had to take the bus. It took me about an hour each way to and from the college. My book bag was extremely heavy, and one day as I was walking back to the house from the bus stop, I felt a sharp pain in my stomach. As soon as I got to the house and walked inside, I fell to the floor. I was alone and in the worst pain. Only a few people knew that I was pregnant. I couldn't walk, so I crawled to the phone and called Tara and her mom across the street. They took me to the hospital, but I ended up having a miscarriage.

At this point in my life, I was seventeen, and I felt so lost. The house went into foreclosure, and my dad permanently moved into his warehouse in Long Beach. My mother was living in a 10-x-10-ft. trailer in Sacramento with her boyfriend while saving money to buy a house. I didn't feel like I had a home. I mean, both of my parents would have welcomed me with open arms, but their circumstances weren't the greatest, and I didn't want to feel like a burden to them any longer.

My relationship was up and down with my boyfriend, not the way it had been before. Lots of cheating and lying, and I was no longer on that pedestal where I felt beautiful and loved. In fact, I felt quite the opposite. I went from feeling confident to having no confidence and low self-esteem. I didn't realize how very wrong what I was going through was. I felt stuck.

2 NEVER A FAILURE, ALWAYS A LESSON

I wanted to finish up that semester of college, as I was exploring what I wanted to be when I grew up. I was enjoying the psychology and sociology classes although my inner self still wanted to open a dance school or a gym somewhere. Essentially, I was still exploring. I finished that semester and failed to get on birth control, so it wasn't that long before I became pregnant again.

My parents had their moments and if anything, they showed me to fight to a fault. Even with their imperfections, they'd tried to stick it out for us. Now that I was pregnant, I wanted to make it work. I would make every excuse in the book for him not treating me well, even at my own expense. I would say hurtful things to myself like, "Well, when he met me, I had a beautiful body, but now I am pregnant, so I don't blame him for cheating and wanting someone more beautiful than me." I was sabotaging myself and pushing the strong, athletic, beautiful girl to the wayside in the process.

I got an apartment with one of my coworkers from Champs and signed a six-month lease as soon as I turned eighteen. My apartment was close to the mall, so I didn't have to travel far. I was glad I had only signed a six-month lease, because my roommate was a little wild. At work, she was calm and sweet, but outside of work, she was quite the opposite. I had the master bedroom since I was pregnant, but we shared bedroom walls, and every night was a party night, if you know what I mean. I didn't sleep much, but I was lucky in that I didn't have any morning sickness at all. My boyfriend never slept over, not one time. We called it off more than once during my pregnancy, but he always said he wanted to be together, and I believed the words rather than the actions.

I was trying to save money to get our own place for when the baby was born. He didn't work and had no desire to work, so I had to carry us all. I didn't see him much during my first six months of pregnancy… just here and there. He didn't go to any of the baby appointments with me. I would just update him after and pretend that he cared. He said he cared, and that he was focused on his rap career so he could support us… and I forced myself to believe it. When I found out we were having a girl, he seemed happy.

I got a second job at a retail store in the mall that worked with my schedule at Champs and helped me save a little money. Working at the mall was great as I had daily cravings for Cinnabon. It was magical to have such easy access to one of the world's greatest delights.

When the lease was up at the apartment, I moved in with my boyfriend and his mom in her one-bedroom duplex. I slept on the floor in the living room since the couch was a hide-a-bed and the bar in the middle of it was terribly uncomfortable. While it doesn't sound too appealing, it was nice for me to share some of what I was experiencing with the father. His mom wasn't home too much during the day, but the bathroom was located in her bedroom, and she would lock her door. I had to try and time it just right every time I needed to use the restroom, which wasn't always easy while pregnant.

The other downside was that I was no longer within walking distance of the mall, and I had to start riding the bus to work. I didn't mind it, except getting home was a challenge. I would typically close the store at the scheduled time of 9:30 p.m. The last bus left the mall at 9:10 p.m. I needed the money, and twenty minutes a day adds up on your paycheck. So on the nights I closed the store and missed the bus, I would have to walk home, or to his moms' home, I should say. It would take about two hours, and I would typically get to the duplex around 11:30 p.m. Sometimes he would meet me half-way, and then it wasn't terrible, because I had company. Other times he would say he would meet me but didn't.

On the nights I had to walk alone, I would reflect on things, and it was healing, in a way. I would think about my parents and my brother and reminisce about Christmas mornings, which had also been Zach's birthday. I'd think about dancing with my dad to Frank Sinatra and riding on the train with my mom. When life felt simple. It seemed like those days were yesterday, yet so far away. The memories made the walk enjoyable. I didn't have a key to the duplex, so I would always have to make sure someone was home.

I vividly remember one night when I walked all that way. I was exhausted: I had worked both jobs that day, my back hurt, and he didn't meet me when he said he would. I got to the house, and no one was there. We didn't have cell phones, and the closest store with a payphone from which I could try and call his friend's house was about an additional twenty-minute walk away. I just couldn't do it. There was a small wooden patio area at the back of the duplex with a brown picnic table. I sat on top of it and began to hear fireworks. It was the Fourth of July. At that moment I knew he wouldn't be coming home anytime soon, and his mother was probably out for the night.

That night I had my first conversation with my daughter. I rubbed my belly and said, "Happy Fourth of July." I asked if she could hear the fireworks and was describing them to her in detail when I would see one in the distance. I was also crying hard, but silently, as I didn't want to wake up the neighbor whose wall was attached to the porch I was sitting on. After waiting over an hour and a half, I decided to walk to where I thought he might be, at a friend's house. It took about forty-five minutes to walk there, which I was only able to do because of the adrenaline and anger. Sure enough, he was there with friends having a great time. He walked me back to the house and simply said he had forgotten to meet me. I was too tired to argue. I was just happy he had a key and I could finally get some sleep.

I came to a realization that night. I didn't feel like a victim, ever. I was very aware that I had put myself in the position that I was in, but I realized that everything I thought I was fighting for didn't exist. How could I have not seen any of this?

At that moment, not truly having a home, I asked myself, "What do I do now? What is best for my daughter? Do I continue to fight?"

The Hustle

I stopped college after my second semester and picked up a third job working the graveyard shift at Del Taco. In my new job, I ran the drive-through line, and my hours were typically midnight to six in the morning. This meant that if I missed the bus from the mall to the duplex, I would have to go straight from one job to the next. A few times, I worked all three jobs in one day. But this was just the beginning of my hustle. My daughter was coming, and I needed to be ready. I was eighteen at the time.

This is where young single mothers often begin to fall into a trap. Many government programs are available but are offered at an incredibly low-income cap. So if you choose to work, you likely don't qualify for those benefits, and if you choose not to work, you may get stuck never knowing your true potential because you didn't go get that job you could have had. You would lose the benefits that you needed… so you just don't try. It's scary. With two minimum-wage jobs, I made too much money. Because of that, my choices were to either quit one job and qualify for several government-assisted programs but be stuck in that low-income bracket, or get a third job to make more money. I opted for the third job.

I met a friend at Del Taco, a young mom with two kids who lived with her boyfriend who was a little older than her. We became close over self-made macho nachos and good conversation as we dealt with the drunks who came through the drive-through. I would occasionally go to her home down the street. I was amazed at what her family had with so little. Her boyfriend worked and helped with the bills, and they had a really small place, but they were also happy. There was no drama, no fancy material things—just a happy family. I envied that peaceful simplicity and easy love.

Meanwhile, in addition to the racism I faced for being with a Black man, I also got stereotyped for being young and pregnant. You would think that people would be kind enough to keep some of their comments to themselves, especially if they don't know you, but they didn't. People would ask me how old I was all the time. Was the father involved? Was I going to be getting married soon? How did my parents feel? These questions would not be asked out of genuine care or curiosity. They would be asked with a judgmental tone, as if they already knew what the answers were and got pleasure out of hearing me say it. My sarcasm would typically take over during those moments, and I'm sure my answers were exactly what they were looking for. My favorite response when asked if the father was involved was that I was trying to still figure out who he was. It was my way of coping with the discomfort and internal shame I felt in those moments. Seeing their reactions made me laugh a little inside.

I have always been a prideful person and have always cared far too much about what other people think of me. I was beginning to love my unborn daughter, feeling her presence and wanting her to feel my strength and to know I was fighting for her future while also shielding her from feeling shame. Every day I felt shamed and judged by every person who stared at my stomach. They didn't have to say anything. I received just as much, if not more, non-verbal cues of shame and judgment. I got it all the time, mostly from strangers, so I shouldn't have cared as much as I did about it. I was just used to being the athletic girl with a six-pack who was destined for success. People used to look at me and admire my physique and feel my confidence, but now they were looking at me differently, with pity and perhaps recognizing my new lack of confidence.

We grow up, and we are conditioned to live our lives in a certain order. You must graduate college, start your career, get married, buy a home, and *then* have children. When you feel judged and worry about the opinions of others, you begin to live for them and not you. You start to live your life based on what you think other people want and what will make other people happy. I knew my situation wasn't ideal, but I didn't want people to project pity on me. I was going to do what I needed to do for my family.

Society places value on perfection. Even before social media, there was a need for acceptance and a desire to be liked by other humans. Social media has exaggerated this need. The desire to fit in and be accepted is stronger now more than ever, and the results are staged presentations of what others feel we ought to be rather than an accurate reflection of who we truly are.

At that stage, I just knew I had my work cut out for me if I was going to prove to my daughter that stereotypes are purely opinions waiting to be shown a new perspective.

Diamond

Once I had saved enough, my boyfriend and I moved from the duplex to a one-bedroom apartment, and his mother came with us to help with the rent. Like in the duplex, his mother had the bedroom, and I would get the living room with my boyfriend and our daughter. This time, there was easier access to the bathroom, so that was nice, at least. I agreed to pay half of the rent and the bills, and his mother would pay the other half. We didn't have a crib yet, and I was buying all I could to be ready. There were just weeks left to go until she would be here. My mom flew down and threw me a baby shower in a hotel room with a handful of people. I was grateful to have been given everything else I needed, including the crib. Finally, I felt ready for her to arrive.

I was still working three jobs. At Champs, I was still climbing up the tall ladder in the back of the store and grabbing shoes, and my co-workers were like family. They cared for me, and when they got wind I was walking home, they would help me when they could. The issue was that they were male co-workers. When they did drive me home, I would have to deal with the jealousy and the arguments simply because a male had driven me home, even though my boyfriend knew it helped me a great deal. I tried as much as possible not to argue and to just stay focused on my daughter.

Her due date came and went. I was beyond ready for her to be here. The doctor told me to be patient, that she would come when she was ready, and they would continue to monitor me. One week past the due date, still nothing had happened.

Two weeks past the due date, I went out to eat at Chili's with Tara and her family and ate a bowl of their chili. When we got back to their house, we were watching television and my back started to hurt… it wasn't too painful; it just felt like I needed to stretch really good. So I started stretching, and it became more and more frequent, and then it was coupled with contractions. Tara's mother began to time the contractions and told me I was probably having back labor.

Back labor? What the hell is that? I thought. That's when I wished I had taken all the free classes offered to me, the ones I hadn't had time for since I was working three jobs. As the contractions got closer, we went to the hospital. The doctors felt I was not dilated enough and said that since it was my first birth it would probably take a while, so they sent me back to the house. As soon as we got back to the house the contractions got even closer and I needed to go right back. The doctors took me right away and set me up in a room. When the nurse came in to check to see how dilated I was, she checked and quickly left the room without saying anything. Then a doctor came in to check me and sharply and firmly told me not to push. Apparently, the baby's body had turned, and she was feet first. Because of this, they needed to do an emergency C-section. I had to quickly sign a bunch of papers, and the next thing I knew, an anesthesiologist came in and I was counting until I fell asleep.

When I woke up after the C-section, I remember seeing one of my coworkers first. Diamond was my first thought, and I wanted to make sure she was OK. He assured me she was and went to grab the doctor for me. The doctor told me that the C-section had been the right move, as the umbilical cord was wrapped around her neck. Had I pushed her out, it could have harmed her. In the meantime, the nurse brought Diamond into the room.

She was perfect, absolutely perfect. As I held her for the first time, it was as if I felt the superpower of a mother's love filling every vein of my body. Any pain I felt, emotionally or physically, didn't matter any longer. She mattered. She was all that mattered to me.

I wanted her name to fit her just perfectly. I knew she would be strong, beautiful, and special. Diamond seemed fitting… and boy was I right!

I don't know if everyone loved the name or not, but I didn't care. Apparently, a movie called *The Players Club* had come out in April 1998 featuring a stripper called Diamond. I had Diamond in January 1999. I hadn't even heard of the movie, but some people thought I had named my daughter after the stripper from the movie. But no, it was completely unrelated. And even if I had, who cares? She fits her name perfectly.

I had to stay in the hospital for a few days. The father eventually showed up and signed the birth certificate. I hadn't realized how much we use our stomach muscles. If I laughed, it hurt. If I cried, it hurt, and coughing and sneezing hurt even more. That shit was painful. I decided to stay with Tara and her family for the first week for extra support. Tara gave me her room, and they helped with anything I needed. My mom, my dad, and Grandpa Ken came to visit me while I was there. I tried breastfeeding, but I was terrible at it. I heard it was good for the baby, so I was trying hard to make it work, with no luck. One day, after trying for four hours, I finally got four ounces! It took me forever, and while that is not very much at all, I was really proud of myself. While Diamond was sleeping, I went to walk downstairs to show everyone what I had accomplished, and I tripped. I caught myself from falling but dropped all the hard work I had just pumped. All four ounces spilled all over the carpet on the stairs. It was both funny and sad at the same time. I was over it—screw breastfeeding! I went strictly to formula after that.

After a week, I went back to the apartment. The place was small, but so was she, and we had everything set up for her. After we'd been in the apartment for just a little over a week, there was a hard knock at the door. When I opened it, three people were standing there, two men and a woman. They asked me if I was Candice, the mother of Diamond, and then asked me where Diamond was. I told them she was sleeping and asked who they were. They showed me papers that explained that they were from some child protective agency and were there to do an emergency check on Diamond. I was confused.

I would never have put her in any danger, nor had she been in any danger at all. They explained they had received an anonymous call and needed to do a physical on her to ensure she was safe and healthy. No one else was home at the time. I grabbed her from the crib and watched closely as they weighed her, inspected her, looked around the apartment, and then left after everything checked out.

I started bawling. Not many people even knew where I lived; I had just moved in. The agency wouldn't tell me where the call came from. It felt like such an invasion of privacy for both me and my daughter. So many people doubted my ability to take care of her, but why? Because I was young? Because her dad was Black? Why? It pissed me off and saddened me at the same time. I grew distant from everyone after that. I had no idea who I could trust anymore.

Diamond's father still wasn't working, and this placed a burden on just getting the essentials. Baby formula was expensive. Every now and then, I would get low on formula, and I would have to steal some from the Ralphs grocery store down the street because I didn't have the money for it and was too proud to ask for help. Many people would have helped me, but I didn't want to look like a failure. My pride prevented me from asking for help when I needed it, and I often suffered unnecessarily because of it. I learned the hard way that it's true that, as the saying goes, closed mouths don't get fed. I didn't want people to feel sorry for me or think I couldn't handle it. I also didn't want to ask the wrong person for help and have that person judge me and think I couldn't provide for my daughter and call CPS on me. I always acted like I had everything under control, and most importantly, I always made sure Diamond was taken care of. This resulted in many nights of buttered tortillas for dinner, but I never felt like a victim... ever. I always knew it was temporary. My desire for achievement never left. The low expectations others had of me never changed the high expectations I had for myself. My priorities shifted, and I was on a new mission to be the best "momdad" (my word for someone who must play the role of both mother and father) I could be. I needed more money, and there wasn't enough time in a day for a fourth job.

I knew I needed a change, and I wanted something better for Diamond. My dad found a great deal on a one-bedroom condo for rent down the street from his warehouse, in Long Beach. He said that if Diamond and

I wanted to come live in it with him, we could have the bedroom, and he was happy to take the couch. The thought of Diamond and me actually having a bedroom sounded great. I spoke to my manager at Champs and found out that they had a keyholder position that had opened up at one of our sister locations closer to Long Beach. It was similar to an assistant manager position, but basically, you hold keys and are often in charge of opening or closing the store. That meant it paid more money. I happily accepted. My father never spent one night in the condo, nor did he ever intend to. He had built a room and installed a shower at his warehouse. He just wanted Diamond and me close, and he knew that if he had told me that it was just for us, my pride would not have allowed me to accept it. Silly me, but thank you, Dad. I broke up with Diamond's father and told him he could call or come see his daughter as much as he wanted, and then I left.

Long Beach

Diamond and I were doing well. Living alone with her for the first time made me realize she was all I needed. I had spent so much time stressing about trying to please others and make everyone happy, when it didn't matter. What mattered was right in front of me. We were fairly close to the beach, and she loved it there. She had a pair of Playskool roller skates I would fit her little shoes in, and I would hold her hands while she pretended to skate; it was one of her favorite things. She loved picking up seashells and wanted to keep literally every single rock and shell she found. She also loved the inside of French fries. I would order fries, tear them in half, and squeeze out the middle just for her pleasure.

I also liked my job. It was easy for me, and I had good hours. I was still at a mall, so if I had the sudden urge for a Cinnabon for old times' sake, it was easily accessible. I also found a kickboxing studio I liked. It was right down the street and had free daycare while you were taking the class. I even got a car, which made a world of difference. I felt like I had so much extra time on my hands simply because I didn't have to take public transportation.

Best of all, I found a good day care provider. The only downfall was that it took me over an hour to get to work and even longer to get back home, with all the LA traffic—though that made me even more grateful for the car. The daycare was in the opposite direction from my job but was reasonably priced, and the caretaker was amazing and worth the drive.

I ended up getting a second job at one of my dad's accounts as a taxi dispatcher. It was a fun job with never a dull moment. I was surprised at how many people called for a taxi instead of calling 911. I once received a call from a woman whose water had broken at a convenience store and who was about to deliver her baby. While talking to her, I realized she had called for a taxi because an ambulance would have cost too much. I was able to keep her calm and she did make it to the hospital in time. It made me grateful that, when I had gone into labor, I had friends around me who were able to take me to the hospital. If I hadn't, perhaps I would have had to call a taxi too.

My coworkers at the taxi company were cool. It was a relaxed environment, and we had fun talking about some of the calls. One day during a break, I met someone who wanted to take me out on a date. I was conflicted. I hadn't ever really been on an official date, and the thought of it made me extremely nervous. After some more thought, I realized it had been a few months since the breakup, and I thought maybe a date would be fun.

I wasn't planning on doing anything sexual the first night, but I still wanted to be prepared and safe. I told the guy at work to give me a couple of weeks, then went to the doctor to get on birth control first. When I arrived at the doctor's office, they gave me a routine pregnancy test to ensure I wasn't pregnant and went over all my birth control options. I was leaning toward the shot, because I knew myself—I hardly remembered to take my vitamins every day, so the chances of me remembering a daily birth control pill were slim to none.

When the doctor came back in, he told me that the routine pregnancy test had come back positive.

I sat there in disbelief. I hadn't seen or spoken to Diamond's father in months, and I hadn't been with anyone else. Diamond had barely turned one, and I had only just started to figure everything out.

Further tests indicated I was just over three months pregnant. I wasn't showing at all; in fact, I was only five pounds over my pre-baby weight, and I had no symptoms. I was even getting kicked and sparring regularly at my kickboxing class, and I still had no clue! Given how far along I was, I only had two options at the time: keep the baby or give it up for adoption. I knew I couldn't go through with an adoption, so I chose to keep the baby.

There was no way I was making enough to support

two kids, but I never thought I couldn't do it. I just needed to figure it out.

I called my dad and told him first. While he was supportive, I could tell he was also deeply disappointed. He had just helped me and Diamond get a place, helped me get a second job, and helped me find the great lady who was caring for Diamond… and here I was at nineteen with baby number two on the way from the same guy who hadn't even purchased a single diaper.

When I called my mom to tell her I was pregnant again, I think she was disappointed, but she also saw it as an opportunity for us to be close again. Shortly after I told her, she called me back and said she knew someone who was hiring for a leasing position at an apartment complex near Sacramento and she had called to see if the manager would be open to interviewing me. It turns out she was because she was also the daughter-in-law of my mom's new husband. While it was awkward for me at first, I flew up to Sacramento for the interview. The manager was great, as was the opportunity. After a successful interview, she offered to hire me at four months pregnant. I felt I could do a good job at what she needed, and I wanted to show her I could do it. The pay was enough for me to only have to work one job, and it would have been silly for me not to take it.

Telling my dad was tough. I knew he would be happy for me. He is so selfless that I knew he would want me to take the opportunity, but I didn't want to leave him in Long Beach, and I knew he enjoyed having Diamond and me around. Of course, he understood and wanted what was best for us and his upcoming new grandchild.

The next morning, after I had given my two weeks' notice, I called my ex and told him I was pregnant and moving. He didn't believe it at first, but perhaps the timing added up to him eventually. He called me back and said he wanted to come with me and Diamond and try for our family. He said he wanted to get a job and help us out and be a better father. It was the first time I had heard him say any of that, including wanting a job, and so I said he could come.

We packed our bags and headed to Sacramento.

3 THE MOVE TO NORTHERN CALIFORNIA

When you drive between Southern California and Northern California, you have to pass over what is called the Grapevine. The Grapevine is a forty-mile stretch of freeway that is so steep that many cars break down each year trying to get through it. While my car was not new, it was a Honda that was in decent shape, and it had good power. I didn't think we would have an issue, until the car started smoking right in the middle of the pass. There were no gas stations and no exits nearby. Diamond was being such a good girl, and while we were in a slight panic over the car overheating, she was in the back seat bobbing her head to the music, refusing to be affected by any of the nonsense we were going through. We ended up having to veer to the side of the road as the engine died. And there I sat, with a car full of everything we owned and a toddler.

I called my mom, and luckily, she had AAA. We had the car towed to the nearest mechanic, which was not very near at all, and the cost of fixing the car turned out to be far more than the car was worth. So we left the mechanic the car, carried what we could—which was basically Diamond and some clothes—went to the bus station, and bused it the rest of the way to Sacramento.

I didn't know which areas of Sacramento were nice or not, but I found a spacious one-bedroom apartment for a really good price. The downside was that it faced the street, but it was within walking distance to a park and a store, and I could live there month-to-month without signing a lease. The carpet was brown, and it smelled a little musty, but Diamond had lots of space to play in. I always saw the good in things, and at least it was ours.

On our second night at the apartment, we heard screams from outside. Then there was a woman banging on our door and begging us to let her in. She said she was going to die if we didn't let her in, so we did. She was frantic and bleeding and told me that her boyfriend (who happened to live next door, by the way) wanted to kill her. I was clenching Diamond, keeping her close to me and protecting her while we called the police. The police came quickly, and there was a lot of commotion outside. The police asked us a few questions, and that was it. I didn't feel safe there any longer. I didn't want Diamond there. I was on the hunt for a new apartment by day three. I had to start my new job the next day, and my mom agreed to watch Diamond at her house, as she had the day off.

When I arrived at my new job, I was extremely nervous. I felt incredibly lucky to have been given the opportunity, and I was determined to show my gratitude. I wanted to be the best employee. I didn't have any leasing experience, but I was used to selling shoes at the shoe store. Leasing came easily to me, and I turned out to be really good at it. I related to people well, and I worked my ass off. The complex was beautiful, what you would consider a resort-style complex. That made it easier. There were two pools, a twenty-four-hour gym, a basketball court, three tennis courts, a business center, a tanning bed, and even a jogging path on the forty-four-acre property. There were just under five hundred units and several different floorplans. I got to the point where

I could tell you the floor plan just by the apartment number, and most of the time, I even knew the resident's last name if it was occupied. I put everything into that job. At times I felt I didn't fit in, though. The ladies there all dressed stylishly, drove nice cars, and had their shit together. Then there was me.

I had no style and cheap clothes. I was twenty years old with my second baby on the way. And I lacked etiquette, but I knew how to talk to people, and I could get them to open up to me fairly quickly. I asked the right questions to help me close the deals, and I just performed. The question I would always ask right away was, "Why are you moving?" That would give me most of the information I needed. If they were just looking and not serious about renting, they would struggle with that question, unless they were a secret shopper, but most of the time they would tell me their whole life story, and from that information, I knew what I needed to focus on when giving them the tour.

The best part of the job was that every morning I would be in charge of making a batch of Otis Spunkmeyer cookies. It would make the office smell amazing, and I had to stay extremely disciplined not to eat cookies all day. The second-best part was that I got to drive around in a golf cart: I thought that was the coolest thing ever. In the winter, the ice would freeze over the sidewalk, and I would race one of the maintenance guys down the hill. Perhaps it was dangerous, but it was super fun!

Once I got settled, I found a doctor. During my first visit, I found out I was having another girl. I had secretly wanted a boy, but little did I know at the time that this was going to be the perfect scenario for me. My due date was set for August. I also got another car, a great $900 deal. It was old, but it ran.

My manager knew I wasn't happy with the apartment I was in and had heard about my crazy neighbor, so she offered me a discount on a one-bedroom unit! I was excited to move into the complex. I felt it would be much safer, and no commute to work was great! I gave my thirty-day notice at my current place and started packing again. Luckily, because we didn't have much, there wasn't much to pack.

I had been shopping around for a day care provider. The boyfriend claimed he was out looking for jobs all day every day, and I was trying to support his effort. I knew he'd met some friends at the park down the street while playing basketball, so I never really knew exactly what he was doing all day. I thought it would be best to find a daycare provider near my job. Luckily, I found one that I really loved. It was an at-home daycare just two miles away. At the same time, Diamond's father decided that instead of continuing to look for a job, he wanted to go back and visit his mom and one of his brothers (who'd been released) in Southern California. He told me he would come back in a few weeks. I took him to the bus station, and my mom helped me move into the new apartment. I was about six months pregnant at the time.

My apartment was a one-bedroom with rose-colored carpet that had a view of one of the pools and the basketball court. Diamond and I shared the bed, and we had a crib right next to the bed for when the new baby came. I spoke to their father here and there, and a few months passed. He still had not come back as the due date got closer.

Deciding what to name my new baby girl was easy. I am a strong believer in karma and things happening as they should. I figured she was meant to be in our lives, so I decided to name her Destiny. Diamond loved to rub my belly and would get excited when she could feel Destiny move. She would rub my belly and say "baby" and hold her baby doll, as if we were both going through the same thing. She was such a character and could not wait for her sister to come. I couldn't either, as I was over being pregnant.

Destiny's baby shower was nice and held at the apartment complex inside the recreation room we had that people could rent. Tara and Shannon traveled to Sacramento to attend, and my coworkers were there. My mom provided the food and the decorations, and we played a few games. It was nice.

As I got closer to my due date, the doctor realized Destiny wasn't turning. As with my first pregnancy, I was told I would need a C-section. Apparently, she was butt first with no intention of moving, and despite all the doctor's efforts to help turn her, she was staying put. At least this time I knew ahead of time and it wouldn't be an emergency operation. The C-section was scheduled for August 7th, which was a few weeks away. I gave their father plenty of notice to ensure he could be there and made sure he knew the date.

In the last two weeks of my pregnancy, I only had four outfits that fit me. I would just alternate the same outfit every fourth day and hope that no one noticed. I worked right up until the day before the C-section. I remember feeling intensely anxious, excited, and nervous. I had not been able to get ahold of their father, so I prepared myself for doing it alone again. At the time, the hospital would only allow the father in the room if you were having a C-section, no other family members or friends. There would be no one to hold my hand and coach me through it like I'd envisioned—just me again.

The next morning, my boss took me to the hospital, as my mom had to stay with Diamond. Diamond's gums had gotten infected overnight, and when she woke up in the morning, her gums were completely covering her top teeth. I was a ball of stress. They needed to get Destiny out, and I wanted to care for Diamond. I was just thankful that my mother could be there for her. So, at the hospital, they ended up caring for Diamond on the third floor while I was on the fifth floor getting ready to have Destiny. I was a nervous wreck.

This time, since it wasn't an emergency, they didn't put me to sleep. Instead, they were planning to give me an epidural. I went into a small room with a heavier nurse who asked me to lean forward toward her while a different nurse gave me a shot in my back. The shot was uncomfortable but not too terrible. After I was given the shot in my back, I was taken to the operating room, where my wrists were strapped to the table for safety. My heart was pounding, and I was scared to death. The previous time, I had already been knocked out by this point, so this was all new to me. Although I was awake, they draped a cloth shield right above my breasts to prevent me from seeing the actual procedure being done. I then heard what sounded like a saw machine. As the doctor went to cut into my stomach, I felt it. I was not all the way numb, and I remember feeling intense, excruciating pain. It was so painful I couldn't even scream. Then I felt cold air hitting the inside of my stomach, and I instantly felt lightheaded, then hot, and I passed out.

When I woke up, the doctor apologized profusely that I had been able to feel the pain. He was sincere and I knew that whatever had happened, it wasn't intentional. I have an abnormally high pain tolerance, but that was by far the worst pain I have ever felt in my life. On a positive note, I was told Destiny came out screaming, which was a good thing, and Diamond had received some antibiotics and was able to come to see me and her new sister in the recovery room.

After a couple of days in the hospital, I needed to

get back to work. Not only could I not afford to go without full pay by going on maternity leave, but I had an opportunity to be the top producer for the company. What better way to show that hiring me pregnant and giving me a chance had been the right choice? I went back to work four days after having Destiny.

The Call

My manager was a blessing. In the beginning, she allowed me to bring Destiny to the office and show people our downstairs model instead of climbing the stairs. I only did that for a short period and then started taking Destiny to day care once she was old enough.

When Destiny turned two weeks old, I received a call from their father. When I answered the phone, he acted as if everything was normal and asked me how my pregnancy was going. Of course, I felt offended. I would rather he had just said, "Look, I only care about me, and I completely forgot or didn't care about you and my daughters but decided I would check on you guys anyway." I don't remember exactly what my curse words were, but you can imagine.

I chose not to tell him about the shitty, terrorizing experience I'd had in the operating room. I didn't want to make it about me. I needed him to know that I was fine, the girls were fine, and I wasn't struggling a bit... even if I was. Then he said he had to go. It would be months before I spoke to him again.

When I started to feel better physically, I started running again. It helped to clear my mind. My coworker's teenage daughter would come over to my apartment and sit with the girls so I could get a quick workout in. Tupac was my favorite running mate, and I listened to "Keep Ya Head Up" on repeat.

Diamond loved being an older sister. She often had trouble saying Destiny's name and would call her Ne-nen-ny. She essentially gave Destiny her nicknames, Nen and Neny. Destiny had a set of lungs on her, and her cries were never soft. It was all or nothing, and she would scream long and hard. Diamond was so caring and would try her very best to get her to calm down. It typically ended up with me putting them both in the car and taking a short drive. Then, like magic, Destiny would fall asleep almost instantly. Once she was in her crib, Diamond and I would stay up a bit longer and watch some cartoons or read a book together before bed.

When Destiny turned six months old, I transferred from my one-bedroom apartment to one of the two-bedrooms on site. After we had moved, I was sitting in the girls' room one night watching them sleep. I loved watching them sleep. I was extra emotional this particular night and crying. I was angry; I was hurt. Although I was technically an adult, part of me still felt like I was a kid raising two kids. I felt like I was doing the best I could, but not having anyone to share these moments with wore on me sometimes. I wanted to tell someone about the bitch at the supermarket who had asked me if I was babysitting and then gave me a dirty look when I told her they were mine, just to know that someone had my back. And I wanted to share the way that Diamond bobbed her head to the beat of any song, and how Destiny could give Mariah Carey a run for her money with her high-pitched crying. I just loved them so deeply, with every ounce of my existence. How could he not love them too?

Looking back now, what I did next makes me want to shake my twenty-year-old self.

Since it was the weekend, I impulsively put the girls in the car and drove to Southern California. He was going to meet Destiny and see Diamond whether he wanted to or not. The drive there was hell. I hadn't planned well. Feeding, diaper changing, gas, and a couple of rests turned a six-hour drive into a nine-hour drive. The most challenging part was when I stopped to pee and had to hold Diamond's hand while carrying Destiny, as I had nowhere to set her down. I completed the toughest squat of my life while holding a baby as I did my business; I refused to place her on the dirty floor. Again, poor planning on my part, as I easily could have carried her in the car seat but hadn't thought about it.

I drove straight to his friends' house, where I thought he might be, and I had guessed right again. It was like nothing had changed at all in his world. Same friend, middle of the day, and no job. I did catch him off guard, and he hugged Diamond. Then I introduced him to Destiny. I didn't have a plan, and I had to drive back because I couldn't afford a hotel. I told him that if he wanted to be in our lives, he could go back with us if he agreed to try to better himself for the girls, and I would agree to try one last time. He hopped in the car. We stopped by his mother's to grab his things and introduced her to Destiny and headed back to Sacramento. He said he was ready to grow up.

When we got back home, I thought it would be nice. The girls would have their dad, and I would be saving money on daycare.

Well, it didn't take long for him to reconnect with a

friend he had met during the brief time we were in the old apartment. When I got home from work, he would take my car and leave to go hang out and not come home until two or three o'clock in the morning. I also started taking the kids back to day care, because I came home for lunch one day at 1:00 p.m. and neither of their diapers had been changed yet. He would stay up late and sleep in late, and they needed way more attention. I was starting to feel like I had three kids. As soon as I got paid, he would hound me for money and tell me all the things he "needed." I always took care of the girls' needs first, but he would get whatever was left, which would leave me with nothing. I had no money to get my hair done, no manicures or pedicures; new clothes were purchased from Goodwill or the swap meet. The situation felt badly wrong, but I kept hoping it would get better.

In addition to all this, my father needed help. Grandpa Ken had lost his battle with cancer. Dad was now running the vending business on his own. He had tried to hire a couple of people, who both ended up stealing from him. So he sold off a few accounts and try to manage the rest by himself. He'd also had a bad fall from the second floor onto the concrete floor of the warehouse, landing on his tailbone. This resulted in some nerve damage and him not being able to feel parts of his leg and foot. The pressure and stress got to be too much, and he began drinking quite a bit. To top it off, he accidentally ran over his dog at the warehouse and had to put her down. He was an emotional mess... understandably.

One night he called me. I could tell he had been drinking. He began calmly telling me how much he loved me and the girls and was apologizing for things he didn't need to apologize for. While I was listening to him, I heard a gun cock through the phone. My dad is not one to play with people's emotions and I whole-heartedly knew he had not intended for me to hear it... but I did, and I acted as quickly as I could. I stayed calm (even though I was screaming and pleading inside) and started telling him about the girls and how much Diamond missed him and how I thought it would be so great for him to be around the girls. I told him that I had moved into a bigger apartment and that I had a bedroom for him all set up and ready to go and that all it needed was him.

That seemed to help a little. Before we hung up, I got him to agree to come and see me and the girls and I made sure he knew we needed him. I was trying my best to give him purpose, hoping it would be enough. I was afraid to hang up with him. As soon as I did, I immediately called my mom. I was shaking as I asked for her help to get him to Sacramento. Although I didn't share all the details of the call, she could tell it was urgent and that he needed our help. The very next day, she and her new husband rented a U-Haul and drove to Long Beach to get him. They put all they could fit in the back of the U-Haul (including my dad on a mattress, as he was in bad shape), simply left the rest, and brought him back to Sacramento.

I put the girls in the master bedroom to give them more space, and I gave my dad the other bedroom, which also had a bathroom right next to it. We put a mattress on the floor in the living room for me and the boyfriend, like the good ole days.

Through all of this, I had a successful year. I started with the company in March, had Destiny in August, and reached my goal of finishing top producer in the company at the end of the year. I never took one sick day.

The girls at this time were into *Dragon Tales*, *Bear in the Big Blue House*, and *Care Bears*. We would sing the songs while I colored with them and they would pretend to be cleaning the house with their fake cleaning supplies. They played incredibly well together, and it was around this time I realized how thankful I was that I had two girls.

Occasionally, they would mess with each other. One time I saw a long, beautiful, curly black lock of hair on the floor. I wasn't sure who had given who a haircut, but my heart sank nonetheless, as I wasn't sure how many more locks of hair I would find. It turned out that it had been Diamond who gave Destiny a haircut, but luckily, she had just taken one good snip, and it didn't look terrible. She was very proud of her haircutting skills and was confused as to why I was so upset about it. Then there were times when Destiny would get jealous when I showed Diamond attention and would give off the biggest fake cry. If I tried to push them both on a swing set, as soon as I switched from Destiny to Diamond, her fake cry would go into full effect. To make up for the attention deficit, I kept the tradition of letting Diamond stay up with me for about thirty minutes longer after I put Destiny to bed.

For the most part, they loved each other and played beautifully together. They loved it when I sang to them, read to them, or watched their favorite cartoons with them.

Changes

I was at work one day when I took this business guy to tour our one-bedroom model. I went through my whole spiel about the complex and took him around on the golf cart to show him the grounds. He told me that he worked for a well-known homebuilder and sold new homes. He said I could do exactly what I was doing with him, but if I got my real estate license, I could show new model homes and make a lot more money.

That night I researched how to get my real estate license and started studying. I made over two hundred flashcards. In our apartment, at the end of our kitchen there was a small closet with bi-fold doors that had the washer and dryer inside it. At night, after the girls had gone to sleep, I would sit on top of the dryer and close myself in that little space for privacy and study for hours. I did this for months, passed the required prerequisites, then signed up for the first available testing date. I passed on the first try.

Then I applied to the same home builder the gentleman had told me about. After the first phone interview, I had to take and pass their personality test.

After that, I had two phone interviews, an in-person interview, and then the last step before getting hired was a home visit. This person would come to your home and talk to you there. I found that odd, but I didn't have much experience interviewing for large companies, so I rolled with it. My home visit was scheduled for three days after my in-person interview went well. They pretty much told me I had the job and went as far as telling me what housing community they planned to assign me to.

Well, we know my living situation was not ideal for having any company. My father had quit drinking again but was right in the middle of detoxing. If you haven't seen a person detox, they sweat profusely, look like they are dying, and are in a lot of pain. My dad describes it as feeling like slowly entering boiling water feet first. Also, it was planned as an evening interview, which meant the girls would be home. I felt slightly embarrassed that our living room was set up like a bedroom, with a mattress on the floor in front of the television. But none of this meant I wouldn't be good at my job, right?

So, the lady arrived at my apartment for my final interview. We sat down at our dining room table, which had originally had four chairs, but two of them had broken, and I placed them to the side to ensure she would sit in one of the good chairs. First, my dad came out to use the restroom looking like he badly needed medical attention. Then at the same time, my daughters decided it was a good time to come out of the bedroom and color on the wall with a red crayon right next to where she was sitting, and their father, instead of trying to save me from death by embarrassment, decided to ignore the situation and turn up the video game that he was playing in the living room… the same room where we were trying to have a conversation. The reason I was given for not being hired was that I didn't have the right personality… but remember, I'd already passed the personality assessment. So that was that.

I didn't want my real estate license to go to waste, so I explored working for a resale company. I found a Century 21 right up the street, and the broker asked to interview me over lunch. He reminded me of Grandpa Ken. He was very much about business but also had a good sense of humor. I was honest and told him that when he came to my house, my home situation was not perfect, but I was a hard worker, nonetheless. I even told him about the last interview just to put it all out there. He chuckled and said he had no desire to come to my home. He said he was a good judge of character and felt

I would be a fantastic addition to his office. He even started me off at a higher commission split because he knew about my situation at home. I was the youngest in the office of a well-established group of Realtors. It was pretty intimidating at first. Just like before, I wanted to show my gratitude, work my ass off, and make some money for me and the girls, and he agreed to show me the ropes. Resale was different from trying to sell new homes. The business doesn't come to you; you have to create your own clients.

It ended up being great timing, because the apartment complex I was working at was being sold and taken over by a different company. The manager who had hired me received a well-deserved promotion as a regional manager for another company, so it was easy for me to give my notice.

At home, my father got sober, and I was happy he had moved up to Sacramento to be with us. The girls' father, on the other hand, kept taking my car and not coming back to the house. I didn't want to screw up my new opportunity, and I really needed the car. He ended up coming home late the night before my first day of work. The next morning when I got into the car to go to work, I noticed footprints on the dashboard of the passenger side. I don't remember exactly how he said they got there, but I knew the whole situation wasn't working. None of it. That weekend, he didn't come home. He didn't have the car this time, so I asked my dad if he could watch the girls for a little bit. I drove to where he hung out and knocked on the door. An elderly man was home. He explained that they had all gone camping, and he told me the campsite name. It was over an hour away. He had been gone two nights already.

I told my dad I would be late, then I drove to the campground in the middle of the night, and I walked to every single campsite until I found the one that he was at. I was confronted by a girl who said, "He likes me because I'm cool." I made a mental note that if that was what cool looked like, I wanted to never be it. He got in the car, and I brought him home. I wasn't crying… I had run out of tears. He needed to go. The next day I took him to the bus station and bought him a ticket, and that was the last we ever saw of him. The girls were one and two years old. I never received any support from him, emotionally or financially. That moment when I dropped him off at the bus station is when I officially became a momdad.

I felt embarrassed and disappointed in myself. Had

I really thought it would be different this time? Sadly, I had. Reality hit once more, and I began to feel like an idiot. And just as quickly as I was about to start with the self-bashing thoughts, I decided I only wanted to pay for the mistake once. I didn't need to re-live the pain or feel sorry for myself because of the situation I ultimately put myself in. What was done, was done, and it was time to move on for myself and the girls.

My mom helped my dad get a job at the train station, and then he got his own place. He loved being with the girls and me, but he was also independent and wanted to feel self-sufficient and to have his own space. The girls and I also had to move again, since I would no longer be getting the discount on the apartment I had. My mother had purchased a rental property in Sacramento and needed a renter, and the timing worked out for me to rent the home from her. It was a three-bedroom, one-bath, 875-square-foot home. The neighborhood was a little rough, but the rent was good, and I found a new day care provider who was close by. She had four daughters and was equally passionate and dedicated as the first one. I was grateful to have met such wonderful people to help care for my girls.

Sometimes when I would take the girls to run

errands, they were a handful. Going to the grocery store was an adventure. Diamond liked to lie on the bottom of the cart like Superman, and I would put Destiny in the seat. Diamond would stay in the cart for the most part but would often find humor in trying to stop the wheels on the cart with any object she could find as I tried to push it. Most often it would be her jacket, and it would get really dirty. Meanwhile, Destiny would try to knock over the stack of apples if I got them within her reach. So, I was always that annoying mother pushing her kids right down the middle of the aisle to ensure Destiny couldn't reach anything.

It wasn't always like that. I would bribe them at times. Don't judge me; it worked. I would tell them that if they behaved, I would let them pick out any toy they wanted from the next store we went to. They didn't know it was the Dollar Store, but it didn't matter to them. Seeing them excitedly shop through the store for a toy was so much fun and it only cost me two dollars.

One of my favorite things to do with the girls was to take them to this park in Midtown that had a pond with ducks in it. I would bring a blanket and some bread, and I would give the girls a couple of pieces of bread each and let them feed the ducks. Diamond would tear the bread into teeny, tiny pieces in an effort to feed every single duck in the pond. By contrast, I would often catch Destiny sneaking off to the side and eating the bread herself. I blamed myself, because I couldn't cook worth a damn.

I didn't learn how to cook from my parents, but they could both cook really well. My mom could cook steak and homemade mashed potatoes like nobody's business, and my dad was known for winning cook-offs with his famous chili. He would also whip up some fried shrimp from time to time, and I would run down the stairs for a plate if I smelled any of that.

I tried to cook, but it's safe to say that I am capable of burning water. Don't get me wrong: I have about three or four things I can make well. But that's about it. The holidays were when I'd feel the worst about it. One extremely broke Thanksgiving, the girls and I had turkey and gravy microwave TV dinners and I put it on a plate and pretended I had made it. Then, as time progressed and I had a little bit more money, I started ordering Boston Market to-go for a few years. The girls were grateful, and they didn't know any different.

Perhaps the best ingredient was the love.

4 EXPLORING

I had good flexibility working as a Realtor, so I decided to take a few more classes in college. I took a psychology class and an English class. I wrote papers about the girls all the time. It was easy to write about them, and it made writing fun. Sometimes I would take them to Burger King down the street, and I would write while they would climb on the play structure. One evening, for the first time, Destiny made it all the way to the top of the structure. She looked down at me from the clear plastic bubble at the top, and waved at me, but then started screaming. I think she had just realized how high she had climbed and was freaked out by it. I was wearing a dress and heels that day, but she would not move, so I had to climb up. Diamond climbed right behind me. As soon as I reached her at the top, she stopped crying and giggled as if she knew how silly I looked. Then, the three of us made it to the slide, and back down we went. After that, she had no issues, and they would both go up and down several times, giving me lots of time to do my homework in peace.

I needed a new car again. The one I had was decent but a little embarrassing and not nice enough to have clients in. I wanted to look more professional. The salesperson who helped me get my car, Calvin, lived at the apartment complex I had previously worked at. I'd seen him playing basketball late at night all by himself through my old apartment window. He would come into the office at times when I was very pregnant. I would always lean forward a bit so my tummy would be hidden behind the desk. I wasn't ashamed of my pregnancy, but I found him attractive and didn't think it would look right to be flirting so late in my pregnancy. Surprisingly, while on the test drive, he told me he was newly single and asked me on a date. We didn't make any plans, but it was the first time I had even given my number out in a long time.

I was also looking online for things to do. I wanted to just meet people in general and wanted to see if there was anywhere I could play volleyball, as I missed playing and competing immensely. I found a place nearby at a softball complex that had sand courts people would play on. I would bring the girls, and they would play next to the court while I was playing on it. The guy who ran the volleyball open courts also held tournaments. This is when I got into playing outdoor grass doubles. I was twenty-three at this time and had never played doubles, but once you get used to it, six people on a court can start to feel crowded. I loved playing doubles, and it became my new hobby. I also found a gym that held open courts where I could practice my skills. I even started refereeing games at night: I would bring the girls to work with me for a little extra cash. I learned so much more about volleyball and met many great people through playing.

The broker I was working for at Century 21 mentored me and taught me so much about real estate. When money was tight for me and I had a closing coming up, he would give me the money early so I could pay my bills. Our office was located in a really good area with expensive homes all around. All the Realtors in my office worked in these neighborhoods. By contrast, I would drive to the areas no one wanted to work in, and I found my niche working with investors from the Bay Area. They would buy two or three houses at a time (equivalent to the same monetary value as one in the neighborhood where my office was), and it was good business for me. I didn't feel scared at all in those neighborhoods. If I showed people respect, they showed me respect. I learned about flipping homes, how to profit, and about the permits and construction that were needed. It was a great experience working with those investors. I worked hard for them, so they stayed loyal to me with their business. In my first year I was awarded the Century 21 Rookie of the Year award.

At the office, I made friends with Sara, the person who was the closest to my age. She was fairly new there. When her mother passed away, I helped her raise money for the funeral, and we became close friends after that. We started hanging out all the time and had a lot of the same interests.

When I got back to the office one day, my boss, Michael, called me into his office. He'd bought me some pepper spray. He said he appreciated my hard work and thought I was doing a great job but also knew the neighborhoods I was working in and wanted me to be safe. I thought it was a thoughtful present. I sat right outside of his office in a cubicle with my back to his office window. When I sat back down at my desk, I decided I wanted to see what color the pepper spray was. I pulled the trash can out from under my desk and sprayed just a little bit of it on a white piece of paper. Immediately my eyes started burning. I quickly pulled the bag out to twist and close it as fast as possible. But it was too late. It was airborne. I was hoping that no one had seen me, but when I glanced slowly and cautiously at Michael, he was looking right at me and shaking his head. My eyes were watering, and then people started coughing and walking outside. That little spray was traveling through the vents. Michael never told on me, and I was never tempted to do that again. That was just one example of him having my back. What he taught me was the type of leader I wanted to be. He was understanding, led by example, had my back when I needed it, and held me accountable when I deserved it. By the way… it was orange.

Business started picking up for me, but the majority of my business was from those two main investors I was working with from the Bay Area. One of the investors, who was in the middle of buying four homes, backed out on all of them because he suddenly didn't have the funds that he needed. The other investor started to hit on me, and that just got awkward. I kept it professional, but he thought I owed him more since he was giving me all his business. He told me I should just date him, as there were several other Realtors he could have been working with. I kindly declined his attempts at dates, and so he no longer wanted to work with me. Then, to make it worse, the market began changing. Banks were going under, people were backing out on sales or not able to show proof of funds, and I needed to have a more consistent income. I was on the hunt for a new job. I loved the flexibility of the work, but the stress of it being commission-only was getting to me. I had to close a deal to pay my rent. One month, I had nothing in the pipeline to borrow from. I had to figure out how to get my rent money. I had a good collection of popular sneakers from when I worked at Champs, and so I went to the swap meet on the weekend to sell my shoes, some clothes, and anything else I could to get enough money for rent. I tried to make sitting at the swap meet all day fun for the girls. I would let Diamond tell people how much things were to buy, and Destiny was content playing with her dolls in the shade.

I raised enough to pay the rent and even had a little

extra leftover, so the following weekend I took the girls to the mall, planning to get them each an outfit. We were walking around one of the department stores when Destiny decided she really liked the way the Britney Spears perfume bottle looked. She picked it up and showed it to me, and I showed her how to smell it, then told her to put it back, and we kept walking. Well, she somehow ended up slipping the bottle into my purse without me seeing her. Just as we were about to leave the store, two loss prevention guys approached me and asked me to come with them as they grabbed my arms. I had no idea what was going on. They brought me back to the office and began questioning me. They said they had me on camera talking to my daughter, and then shortly after, her placing the perfume bottle into my purse… as if I had plotted with my five-year-old to steal!

I wish I had known then what I know now, because of how inappropriate they were. My girls were crying. I had more than enough cash on me to pay for the cheap bottle of perfume, but they wouldn't let me pay for it. I couldn't even wear perfume, as it gave me headaches, but they didn't know that, nor would they believe me. I refused to sign a document stating I had stolen it. Then the cops came. After watching the video, they ended up letting me go, but it was scary. Part of me was thinking it might be karma for all the baby formula I had stolen back in the day. But that day I hadn't stolen anything, nor would I ever teach my daughters that. When the girls and I got back to the house, I felt defeated, embarrassed, and angry. Karma or not, I was trying to be the best mother I could be, but I felt like I was constantly having to fight. Fight for respect, fight for love… just fight.

Meanwhile, I started taking Diamond to speech therapy. She was struggling with pronouncing a few of her letters. I took her to a nice place near my office that had been highly recommended by her teacher. I will never forget the first day. Diamond was excited to go. The session was going to be with me and Diamond and another mother and her son. Diamond and I arrived first and waited with the teacher. When the son and mother arrived, the son stopped walking toward the table when he saw Diamond. He did not want to sit with us. When the teacher asked the boy what was wrong, he pointed at Diamond and said, "I don't like her; she's brown."

Now, I had experienced racism from the perspective of a White mother raising two little Black girls, and also as a White woman who was dating a Black man, but this was the first time I had experienced racism being directed at my daughter, and it felt so much worse. It was painful.

The White mother immediately responded, "Oh, I don't know what he's talking about. We have friends that color."

It was clear to me where the boy had learned it from.

It went completely over Diamond's head. She had no clue what was going on. She just wanted this boy to sit down so we could get started.

He eventually sat down reluctantly and clung to his mother as if we were going to bite him.

Throughout the whole session, I focused on helping with Diamond's therapy, but internally I was angry. It wasn't the boy's fault; he had learned it. I felt sorry for him. I hoped that even if he was being conditioned to think that way, he would also be taught through experiences as he got older not to judge people based on their skin tone. That moment made me realize I didn't want the girls to go to school out there. I had thought it would be better because of the nice neighborhoods, but it was not diverse at all. What if the next time it didn't go over Diamond's head, and the next ignorant kid judged her for being Black and hurt her? I decided that after first grade, I would switch their school to something more diverse. Some people felt this decision was a bit premature: but I thought about Tanika that day and how I was Diamond's age when I was best friends with her. I was surrounded with diversity growing up, and I wanted the girls to be also. While the school and area were fantastic, the majority of the students were Caucasian. I didn't want my girls to feel judged purely because their beautiful skin tone was not the same as everyone else's.

Outside of school, I did my best to keep them sociable. I took them to most places with me, and they both had their favorite birthday spots. Diamond's birthday is in January, so we would have to be indoors: she would always choose Chuck E. Cheese. She loved that place! Destiny's birthday was in August, and she would always choose this place called Funderland. It is a small outdoor amusement park with rides for young kids. They both went to Chuck E. Cheese and Funderland for at least four years in a row. It made birthday planning easy for me.

I would also often take the girls to Barnes and Noble with Suzi, a friend I had met through volleyball who was also a single mother. She and I would sit at one of the kid tables in a corner and talk while the kids spent over an hour looking at books. It was a good way to have adult girl time and to see what books the kids were into. Most of the time we wouldn't buy a book, but occasionally we would if they expressed heavy interest in one. They enjoyed books and liked it when I read to them because I would try and read them with expression to make it sound exciting. *If You Give a Mouse a Cookie* and *Green Eggs and Ham* were two of their favorites.

I would often write poems about the girls and enter them in contests I saw on flyers. I chose to submit a poem to this one ad I saw and found out shortly thereafter that it had been chosen to be published in a poetry book. The poem was dedicated to my daughters and was called "A Single Mother's Strength."

A Single Mother's Strength

Things happen for a reason
I don't think about the pain,
My struggle is their survival
Their happiness is my gain.
Their dependence on me,
Is how I maintain.

I live for their smile
And creative imagination,
As I watch them sleep

I thank God for this creation.
Their future,
Is my motivation.

I'm mom, I'm dad
I'm fearless in their eyes,
My tears at night
Will always be disguised.
Their voice in the morning,
Takes away my cries.

Because of them
I am me.
Because of me
They will see,
That against all odds,
We can still succeed.

The Car Salesman

One night when my mom had the girls for a sleepover, I finally ended up going on a date with Calvin, the guy from the apartment complex who asked me on a date during the test-drive. He was tall and had a darker chocolate completion and an athletic frame. He had his own apartment and made good money, and we had a lot of the same interests, mostly sports.

We started seeing each other regularly. He had left the dealership to work at a gym as a manager and personal trainer. The downside was that the job was over an hour away, so he'd moved into his parents' house in the Bay Area. When we decided to make it official, after dating for about a year, he moved in with me and the girls. As I was protective of them, we had many talks beforehand to ensure he knew what he was getting into. In fact, he told me that in his past relationship, the woman had had a daughter and left him. It broke his heart because he had been attached to the kid and would never want that to happen again. When he moved in with us, he was supposed to transfer from the gym he was working at in the Bay Area to the same-franchise gym by our house. He said it was going to take about a month, so I agreed to help him with his bills that month during the transition, but then the transfer didn't happen. This is when he decided he wanted to try to go pro in boxing. He was fully aware of my financial situation but had me convinced he could go pro if he put all of his time and effort into training at a new boxing gym he'd found in Sacramento.

I should have listened to the little voice inside my head at the time, but I didn't. Instead, the girls and I got attached to him. I thought we would get married, as he lived with us for two and a half years. I loved his family, and they loved the girls and me. He only helped me pay rent one time. Also, he wasn't faithful, which completely broke down my self-esteem again, to the point that I thought I should be grateful that a man wanted to be with me when I had two kids— "baggage," as he put it. He was a fantastic manipulator and my ass fell for all of it. I truly believed he was the greatest thing for me and the girls and that things would be better.

My childhood friend Tara had found love and asked me to be her maid of honor at her wedding. I didn't have a lot of money and couldn't afford to fly, so we drove with the girls. Calvin came with me to help me with the girls so I could be there for her during all the wedding stuff. We got to the hotel and unpacked, and then he asked if he could use the car to go see a friend for a bit. I said sure, but he didn't come back until the next day, right before we had to go to the venue for the rehearsal. I was up all night, feeling utterly stressed. I didn't know if he was cheating or something had happened to him. He told me he had been visiting this female friend of his and it had just gotten too late to drive back. I showed up to the rehearsal feeling like the wind was knocked out of me but doing my best to be there for my friend and to be happy, for her sake. The wedding was later that day. I didn't get a chance to nap, and right as the wedding started, I was feeling flushed and lightheaded. I remember I was lined up with the bridesmaids at the altar. The bride looked beautiful and I was holding the ring, waiting for my moment to give it to her. But just before it was time to give her the ring, I knew I was about to pass out. I turned, gave the ring to the girl behind me, and exited from the back before immediately passing out on the stairs. I honestly don't remember much after that. I know we finished the wedding, I did give my speech, and we drove back.

And still, I stayed with him.

He started to be more supportive and came with me to a few events the girls had. Diamond was in a talent show, and I had choreographed a dance for her to Ciara's song "1,2 Step." It was adorable, and she did great. He brought her flowers. It was nice to have someone to share those moments with. He watched cartoons with the girls, tried to teach them manners, and would take us to the arcade to play a few games. He was doing far more than their father had ever done, so in my eyes, this was a good thing for us all.

One evening my mother was watching the girls overnight while I played in an all-night volleyball tournament that only took place once a year. In the middle of the night, I received a call from my mom. She started the conversation off by saying, "Don't get upset…" Naturally, I immediately started asking what happened. She told me that Diamond had told her that my mom's husband had kissed her funny. Diamond had said that, while Destiny was in the bathroom, he had asked her to snuggle with him and asked her to give him a fishy kiss (where you pucker your lips out like a fish). So, she puckered her lips, but rather than just briefly touching her lips back, he had sucked the outside of her lips, gave her a cookie, told her she was a good girl, and asked her not to tell anyone. She was smart enough to know that was wrong and brave enough to say something about it.

I immediately forfeited the tournament and left to pick up the girls. I grabbed the girls and never went back to the house after that. My mother knew she was welcome to see the girls; we would just have to meet somewhere, or she could come to our house. I know it was hard on my mom, too, and I was glad she told me right away.

I asked Diamond many questions that night. "Where were his hands? Was that the first time he made you feel uncomfortable? Did anything else happen?" Thankfully, that was the first and only time she had felt uncomfortable with him.

He swore up and down that he would never do anything like that to Diamond and that he had given her a cookie because she was being so good. My mother, who was torn about what to do, paid to have him take two different polygraph tests. He passed both, indicating he had no sexual desire toward Diamond. Even so, what mattered to me, was how Diamond felt. If she felt uncomfortable, I knew I would never take her back over there and put her in that situation, so I didn't. We never saw him again after that night. My mom ended up divorcing him and moving to Florida to take care of Grandma Hazel when she was diagnosed with Alzheimer's.

Calvin was protective of the girls, especially after that. He taught them things like never to sit on a man's lap and other things from a man's perspective that I wouldn't have thought about, and I appreciated that. He did discipline the girls at times and would spank them occasionally. One day we drove out to the Bay Area to see his family. He and the girls visited his parents, and I went with his sister to run some errands. I had always wanted a sister and loved hanging out with his sisters whenever I could. When we got back to his parents' house, his mother was visibly upset. He had spanked Diamond while l was gone and left a cut on her bottom.

I was beyond upset and angry. I was yelling and cursing at him in front of his parents and told him he would never lay a finger on them again and that I would do all the disciplining from then on. He said he didn't mean to cause the cut, but I didn't care. You can spank a child and have it be effective without breaking the skin. He had gone too far, and whether he had intended to or not, I needed to protect my daughter. I gave her a warm bath while we were there and made sure she was OK before we headed back home.

He never spanked them after that, but things between us were getting worse. I was never big on spanking. We would argue, because he felt they needed it at times, whereas I would go have a conversation with them instead. He would tell me I was a weak White mother who didn't know how to discipline and raise Black children. It's not that I was against spanking. I had been spanked; most people I knew were spanked... I had just made a decision not to do it any longer. The girls were six and seven at the time.

A few months later, things seemed to be stable between us. I was going to meet my mom in Reno for her fiftieth birthday. It was only an hour and a half away from me. I planned to drive up, celebrate with her, and go back home in the morning. I asked my close friend from work, Sara, to go by the house and help with dinner that night and to check on the girls. The plan was for her to help with dinner, then help put the girls to bed and go home. When I got back, I walked in the door, and the girls ran up to me, excited to see me. Then I went to my room to put my stuff down. When I opened the door, Calvin was in the room crying. I knew nothing had happened with the girls because I had just seen them. He closed the door behind me, held me so I couldn't move, covered my mouth, and told me that he'd had sex with my friend while I was gone. He said, "Sorry, it just happened."

My heart hurt deeply. Sara and I had been so close. How could she? How could he? I kicked him out, and then I called her and cussed her out. I wanted them both out of my life.

I was left feeling like a failure as a mother. When I had met the guy, he had all his shit together and seemed like a great person. I must have this sign on my forehead that reads, "Hey, I will support you... Just don't work and treat me like shit." It seemed to be my pattern.

So it was back to me and the girls again. Which was fine with me. At least now I could put just my name on all the Christmas presents I'd bought, and I wouldn't have to walk on eggshells any longer. It felt both sad and liberating at the same time.

We tried to remain friends, as the girls missed him, although that didn't last long. The very first time he came to see us after we broke up, he went through my belongings, found a photo in my camera of me watching the Lakers game with friends, and because there were two males in the group photo, he decided to take a hammer to all my jewelry and placed all my underwear in the bathtub and pissed on them... all of them. I had also just had nose surgery to correct the deviated septum I'd gotten from a poorly executed monkey bar jump I attempted when I was ten that broke my nose badly. Calvin chucked a full Gatorade bottle at me from across the room and it missed my nose by less than an inch. I still had the cast on my nose from the surgery and had that Gatorade bottle hit me, it would have been devastating. The girls were not home yet when all that happened, but I decided that it was best he stay out of our lives after that. He left and I cleaned up the mess and the girls never even knew he was there.

Hampton Court

My boss, Michael, had passed away unexpectedly from a heart attack. The new broker that replaced him made it clear he would not issue any cash advances, even if we had for-sure deals in the pipeline to close. I didn't want to be there any longer anyway. I didn't want to see Sara at the office after what she'd done to me, and with Michael gone, it felt different. I had been applying for numerous jobs and ended up getting hired as a property manager at an apartment complex called Hampton Court. It only paid $600 a month, but it included a rent-free two-bedroom apartment, so I took it. The apartment complex was older and nothing like the resort-style complex I had worked and lived at before, but the area was far more diverse, and I liked that part of it. And the elementary school they were going to attend was just down the street.

The girls and I got to know all our neighbors pretty quickly. I soon learned the downside of being the property manager who lives at the complex: everyone knocks on your door for everything. They knock to tell you about a running toilet, to let you know their rent may be late, and sometimes to pay their rent. It took me a couple of months to slowly condition everyone to not knock on my door and to just see me at the office… unless, of course, it was fire, flood, or blood. I felt it was safer for the girls that way, and I wanted my time with them to not be interrupted so frequently.

The girls and I have many memories of Hampton Court. It was the first time I had been able to paint their room. I painted it light purple and light sea green and added a little wallpaper border halfway up the wall. It was a dual-master plan, meaning the apartment had two master bedrooms and they had plenty of space, each with a walk-in closet. I would often find one of the girls sleeping in the closet, pretending it was a separate bedroom.

We also discovered that Destiny was allergic to olive trees and Bermuda grass one day when she came inside from playing with her friends and her eyes were swollen shut. I took her to the doctor and got her tested. Unfortunately, there were olive trees and Bermuda grass all over the complex, so she had to be more cautious of where she played after that.

The girls made a few friends at the complex. One little girl lived with her blind father. He hadn't always been blind, but he had unsuccessfully tried to kill himself, which had caused his blindness. He would fearlessly dive into the pool as if he could see, and he could get around pretty well without help. His daughter was abnormally mature for her age and was in charge of cooking and cleaning around the house. Because of that, their apartment was pretty dirty, and I would often call the family member listed on the application to come and assist with the cleaning and help the daughter out. She was incredibly smart and in unfortunate circumstances.

The girls also made friends with two younger boys who lived on the upper level. One day when I was off work, I realized all of their LEGOs were gone. The girls had given all their LEGOs to these boys. Initially I was upset, because LEGOs weren't cheap, but then it made my heart happy that they'd given something they liked to play with to these boys who didn't have as much.

After about six months as the manager, I realized $600 was not enough to pay my bills and get the girls the things they needed. I needed more money. There was one evening in particular where I felt extra sad. It was the day before payday, and people who live paycheck to paycheck know that the day before is the worst: it's always when you are the most broke. It was around 5:00

p.m. when a sound that every kid loved could be heard from a distance and getting closer: the ice cream truck. But I didn't have the money. I didn't even have $2 to buy them ice cream. I didn't want the girls to know and so I quickly ran to the radio and turned it up really loud and started dancing with the girls. I left the music on for a few minutes to block the sound of the ice cream truck. They didn't have a clue, and while I had fun dancing with them, I felt sad about the ice cream. Moments like that would motivate me to strive for better.

Coincidentally, the company I was working for was looking to hire a regional manager. The requirements for the position were a bachelor's degree and a real estate license. I had the license but not the degree yet. So I lied on my resume and said I had graduated from Long Beach State. I ended up getting the job and started overseeing six apartment complexes. I was also still managing the place I lived at, but I kept it fully occupied, so it was easy to manage. We didn't need a person in the office. I also still got to keep my free apartment, which was even better. As a regional manager, I only got paid about $30,000 a year. That is extremely low for a regional position, but they took a chance on me, and by now you know I express my gratitude with loyalty and hard work.

This management company was run by an incredibly strong woman, Alice, who took no crap from anyone. She was older, but no one dared ask how old. We all guessed mid-seventies. She was fierce and taught me a lot about the business and how I wanted to be—and not be—as a leader. It was a small company that managed forty-four apartment complexes. With our company being so small, I did many other tasks such as HR duties, talent management, budget writing, held all-company meetings, and learned how to lead and manage people twice my age and gain their trust (which wasn't easy).

About a year later, the other regional manager decided to retire after working for the company for eighteen years. I took over the management of his properties. I was given the properties that required the most attention since our president and the vice president needed to focus more on the business. While Alice was feisty, she also had a big heart and was helpful when it came to the girls. If the girls had to stay home from school because they were feeling ill, I could bring them to the office and just close my office door and make them a cozy space so I would not have to take the day off work. She also never gave me trouble for needing to leave early for their school events, as she knew they were important to me. Employees were loyal to Alice, and many of them had been there for over ten years.

I would end up spending nine years with the company before I decided I needed to move on. By that time, the girls were needing more, and I felt I had given a good amount of time to the organization. I am grateful for all I learned from my time there and the way that Alice helped me grow as a leader. My main leadership lesson working for Alice was inclusiveness. In every leadership position I have held, I have incorporated inclusiveness to create a much stronger level of engagement. Trust and respect are built much faster that way. Alice passed away seven years later, and all the same employees that had been there when I worked for her were there at her funeral. She meant a great deal to many people.

Online Dating

It had been a long time since I had gone on a date, and my single-mom friend, Suzi, had found love on an online dating site. She decided to set me up with a profile and completed all the information for me, so I agreed to try it out. I hadn't really believed in the online dating thing until she found love through it, and then I thought, "Sure, I'll give it a try." At first, I wasn't getting matched with anyone I was interested in, but one day I finally did. He was in the military and was overseas in Germany at the time. It was convenient because I didn't want to feel pressured to see anyone in person right away and didn't want anyone around the girls too soon. The nine-hour time difference also worked out because I could call him after the girls had gone to bed and it didn't interfere with my time with them. I didn't get much sleep, but that was OK.

What I liked about him was that he challenged me intellectually. He had traveled and experienced quite a bit, and it was nice to hear about the world outside of my mommy bubble. I hadn't experienced much, and he was able to tell me a lot I didn't know. He was also the first White guy I had dated and was over six and a half feet tall. After virtually dating for about six months, we talked about getting engaged and me potentially moving with the girls if all went well. Even writing that sounds funny, but trust me, when you are in it, it feels way different. He was coming to visit. His best friend lived in San Francisco, so the plan was for him to fly into San Francisco, spend one night there, and then come to see me the next day.

When he arrived, I was nervous. He made good money. I didn't… but I acted like I did. I would not have lied if he asked me, but I don't think he cared about that either. I just didn't want him to think I was searching for a guy to take care of me and the girls (because I wasn't), so I acted like I could hang with him financially. Although I had the girls meet him, we mostly hung out alone just to get to know each other in person. He went back to the Bay Area for a few nights, then came back before going back home. I bought tickets for a murder mystery dinner and we went out that night. Earlier that day he said he needed some clothes, so I took him to the mall. I will never forget that he spent $700 on two shirts and a pair of pants at Nordstrom. They were a name brand I don't even remember. At that point in my life, I hadn't spent that much on clothes in total.

While we were walking around the mall, he kept getting text messages that were making him laugh and smile. I thought it was rude, since we didn't have much time together, but then he told me why. Apparently, while he was visiting his friend, he had gone out and they had been with some gal friends. They were texting him funny things about the night they went out, and he was sharing it with me. He told me that they thought it was silly he was on an online dating site and how they had played games like "Would You Rather?" and "Two Truths and a Lie." It made me feel like he was ashamed to have met me online, and I wasn't familiar at the time with the games he was referring to due to my mommy bubble and lack of social experiences. He also boasted about the super-nice place these girls were renting in San Francisco, which made me feel ashamed of my OK apartment. I don't think he was intentionally making me feel that way; I felt that way due to my own insecurities and situation.

The murder mystery dinner was fun, but something felt off. I didn't know if it was because I was secretly irritated that he had been hanging out with these girls who also had his number now, and he was clearly happy about it. Or was it my intuition? All I know is that I felt sad on the inside. To no surprise, he told me that night that he wasn't ready and that he still loved his ex-wife, and he left. I later discovered he ended up marrying the girl who was texting him while we were at the mall.

While the girls didn't really get to know him and I had done a decent job at keeping some distance, I couldn't help but feel like a shitty mom… again.

It's hard dating as a single mother. You can't just freely go out when you want to, and everything must be planned. You don't want to introduce someone to your kids until you think it is serious, and even then, it can backfire. The girls didn't know their father, my relationship with Calvin had ended roughly, and now this. At this point, the girls were nine and ten. I didn't go back on the dating site. I was fine staying single until they were older. I decided to just focus on work and our future. Besides, I liked being celebrated on both Mother's Day and Father's Day.

The girls were starting to need more. Destiny needed braces. My insurance didn't cover braces, so I had to sign up for monthly payments. She also needed glasses, and while insurance covered most of that expense, it was still tough to come up with the rest.

Risky Move

I started to look for new opportunities and felt confident I could find something decent with all the experience I had gained. I saw an ad on Craigslist for an area manager position with a new startup company. I applied for it and initially interviewed with the recruiter. After that, she set me up with an in-person interview the following week.

I arrived at the interview, which was at a Starbucks in a rougher part of town. I knew the company didn't have an office yet, and it was a public place, so I rolled with it. The interview went well until about forty-five minutes into it, when he told me he had filled the position I was applying for about a week ago. He noticed that I had my real estate license and asked if I would be interested in being a leasing agent with their company. He added it had the potential of paying me more than what I would have received as an area manager, since the leasing agents get a commission.

It was a tough decision. The salary was only $20,000 a year, but the income potential was extremely tempting, given how good I was at leasing. The downside was that I had earned a regional manager position at the age of twenty-three, and I had been working my ass off for the past nine years. So going from a regional position to a leasing agent again was like sliding all the way down the totem pole in the property management industry. I enjoyed leading teams and being part of the decision-making process for the organization; it would be a tough transition for me. I would have to climb all the way back up… if the title and position were important to me.

At the moment, I needed money. So, I decided to take the job and kept my regional job until I had made enough with the new job to quit. The hours I was working were insane, but I needed to make sure I could make enough to provide for me and the girls. I worked both jobs for an entire year before leaving my regional position. In the end, it was the right decision, because I was earning $100,000 a year. Much lower job title, but a lot more money. With my first big commission check, I Googled Ralphs grocery store headquarters. I then went and obtained a money order in the amount of $300. I estimated that to be the amount of baby formula I'd stolen from them back in the day, and I added a little extra for interest. I then mailed it from a post office box in the Bay Area. I simply put 'for Enfamil' in the memo section. I knew it didn't excuse the fact that I'd stolen, but being a heavy believer in karma, it was something I had wanted to do for quite some time.

What I loved most about the new job was that I had all the flexibility in the world to make my own hours, for the most part. I was able to stay involved in the girls' activities and be a member of the school site council. I helped organize the talent shows and dances, and I never missed an event. The girls were very familiar with my job, as I would often have to pick them up from school and have them do homework in the car while I showed homes, or they would show them with me (if I knew the client well). They would pretend the home was theirs and would call out their bedrooms and tell me how they would decorate. They even learned property management lingo. Destiny once told me jokingly during a showing that if we rented the home, we would have to pay a pet deposit for Diamond. It was fun. Until... I started running out of homes to lease.

Leasing out a home was similar to showing homes to sell. I would make sure I knew about the neighborhood, schools nearby, anything that would help rent it. We had homes in great areas and not-so-great areas, but I was used to the less desirable areas from selling homes, so it didn't bother me. We had a plan with the maintenance guys that we would always leave the blinds open at a forty-five-degree angle. If I pulled up to a home and all the blinds were closed, there was likely a squatter in the home.

One day I pulled up across the street from the house I was showing and waited for my clients. When they arrived, they pulled up and parked right in front of the home. I got out of my car and walked over to introduce myself, but just as I approached their car, I noticed a pit bull in the middle of the street just staring at me. No leash, no owner nearby, and it started running straight at me. My instinct was to open up the back door of the client's car and jump inside. I didn't close the door fast enough, and the pit bull jumped inside the car with me! Protecting my face and expecting the worst, I rolled up into a ball. The pit bull started licking me and was nothing but friendly. It still scared the shit out of me and made for a memorable showing.

Another time, it was my day off and a random client called and said she wanted a quick move-in and needed to see a house that evening. I was just finishing cooking dinner for the girls, I was forty-five minutes away from the home she wanted to see, and it was already seven o'clock at night, so I asked if it would be OK if I met her there in the morning. She said no, she needed to see it tonight and would just call my company and get someone else to show her if I was unwilling. Never wanting to throw away money, I quickly finished cooking dinner and had my neighbor watch the girls. I was wearing dark blue jeans and a black sweater. I had a pair of slip-on black boots with fur inside that I slipped on quickly, and then off I went to keep this client happy.

When I got to the house, I introduced myself, and she immediately started taking notes… on me. I had been in the business long enough by then to know that I was dealing with a secret shopper. Internally I was pissed, because this woman had taken me away from dinner with my girls to make her secret-shopping quota for our company. In the past, I would hire these secret shoppers myself to go pretend they were looking for apartments to see how our managers and leasing agents were doing. I knew the questions I would get asked and planned to still perform a good showing to ensure my company knew I was doing well for them. Occasionally, there is a shopper who unfortunately only looks for the bad in the people they are secretly shopping. She first tested me with fair housing questions that I knew how to answer with ease. She then told me she didn't want the house because it was on a busy road and had a window in the closet. I still went for the close (as that is also part of the scoring), and I offered to show her more homes nearby and she declined. I did all I could and felt I performed well. When the results came back about a week later, she noted in her report that I had showed up to the appointment with slippers on and had not wanted to show her the home that evening. Of course, neither was true, and my company knew me well enough to know I wouldn't show up to a home in slippers or turn down money, but I still took it personally. Companies rely on secret shoppers to provide them with honest, unbiased feedback. Her comments could have gotten me written up—or worse—had my company not known me as well as they did.

The new company was growing rapidly, and they continued to expand in many markets, but not California. We didn't have as many homes to lease any longer, and my commission checks were getting lower and lower. My base salary was still just $20,000. Needing more income, I started doing hybrid roles with the company. First, I became an assistant property manager, while also leasing. That gave me a slightly larger salary, and I would still make some commission. From there, I moved up to property manager and still did leasing, but eventually, I had to stop leasing due to the added responsibilities in the office. But at least my salary was enough to cover my bills, and my job still allowed me the flexibility I needed to be involved with the girls' school activities.

5 DOING IT ALL

The girls participated in many activities in elementary school. They made the dance team, and Diamond sang one of her favorite India Arie songs in the talent show. They loved the book fairs and fundraisers. I would hustle hard trying to get them to have the most fundraising sales, just for them to earn a prize that was probably worth about ten bucks... but it made them feel special.

Diamond won first place at the science fair with a project we enjoyed. Using specific notes on the keyboard, she drank different liquids to see if it was easier or harder to sing specific notes after each. We used water, Gatorade, milk, orange juice, and soda. It was a fun project and popular at the science fair.

When the girls were in fourth and fifth grade, they

played basketball for their after-school program. They were both aggressive on the court, and I was that mom who would run up and down the court shouting the whole time. I am confident I annoyed both the refs and the coaches. Diamond also wanted to play football. She had a really good arm, so she tried out for the football team and ended up being their quarterback. The coach, Mr. Jon, was one of the after-school program teachers. He had a smooth, caramel complexion and a nice smile. He was also good with the kids and had good energy. Sometimes when the girls got in trouble, he would have to talk to me about it when I came to pick them up. Let's just say… I didn't mind at all. Not quite to the point where I wanted the girls to get in trouble, but almost.

After that school year ended, the girls went to visit my mom in Florida for two weeks. I was incredibly bored without them and decided to Facebook friend-request all the after-school program teachers. You know, I didn't want to make it too obvious. It worked. I received a message on Facebook from Mr. Jon the next day, asking if I wanted to go hang out sometime. Taking full advantage of the girls being gone, I was super excited to have plans. I happily accepted.

For our first date, we trespassed. I wasn't sure what

to expect, but I rolled with it. We hopped a fence at a place he had previously worked at that had a pool and some tennis courts. We shared a bottle of Malibu Rum, I finally learned how to play "Never Have I Ever," and then we went skinny-dipping.

Don't judge me.

You already did, but that's OK.

When I had agreed to hang out, I hadn't thought it would be a regular thing. I truly was content being single and had accepted that I likely would not have a partner in life until the girls were older. I treated that first date like a YOLO moment. However, he asked to see me again before I went to go get the girls from Florida. We didn't break any laws on the second date, and it was much more relaxed, but we did have a great time and good conversation. The next morning, he was leaving for a road trip to San Diego with friends. I was leaving in two days to fly to Florida and then fly back with the girls.

The next day, I received a call from my mother telling me that Destiny had been in a bicycle accident. She had been racing my mom and Diamond on a gravel road with flip-flops on, and one of her flip- flops had got caught in the wheel, which caused her to flip off her bike. When she landed, she landed on top of the bike and on the handlebars, which were sideways, sticking straight up. She was taken to the children's hospital, where they found out that she had torn her kidney upon landing. She had to stay in the children's hospital for a week with her head and heart angled lower than her feet. When she was released, she could not fly, so I decided we would take the train back. It would be a seven-day trip, but it was the best option.

The three of us had a room on an Amtrak train. If you have a room, your meals are covered. If you haven't traveled by train before, do it and get a room. It is a great experience and a good way to enjoy time with your family. Destiny and I shared the bottom bed, which was a little larger, and Diamond slept in a bed that pulled down from above. We had an eight-hour layover in Washington, DC. We got off the train, and I pushed Destiny in a wheelchair and took them both to the Smithsonian Museum. We walked around the outside of the White House before making our way back to the train. We were going to have to change trains in Chicago. When we arrived in Chicago, the conductor told us that since the train was running so far behind schedule, they were going to put us up in a hotel for the night and we would be catching the next train in the morning.

We took that opportunity to explore Chicago for the day, with me still pushing Destiny in the wheelchair. We had the best build-your-own deep-dish pizzas, then Diamond and I played in a volleyball tournament we stumbled upon. We saw the *Married with Children* fountain and walked back to the hotel. We loved that day in Chicago, and the three of us still talk about wanting to go back and visit again.

We eventually made it back home, and my employers were happy I was back. Destiny had to take it easy but was able to make a full recovery.

We were also able to go back to one of our traditions. Every Sunday the girls and I would meet up with a group at a public kitchen and cook food for the homeless. Then we would transport the food from the kitchen to Cesar Chavez Park in downtown Sacramento, where we would make plates of food for about 130 homeless people who would show up like clockwork at 1:00 p.m. I encouraged the girls to have conversations with them, and we would make a plate for ourselves and eat with them. This helped the girls to gain an appreciation for what little we had and showed them that we shouldn't judge others without really knowing their story. Many of them had amazing stories.

Chongo was one of my favorites. He'd chosen to be homeless. He was an author, had his own website, and was featured in *The New York Times* in 2008 for his rock-climbing ability. He jokingly would tell the girls and me that he felt bad for us because we had to sleep in the same spot every day, whereas he got to choose his home daily. Chongo reminded me that the quality of our life depends on the quality of our thinking. My perception of Chongo's reality didn't matter. To Chongo, he was in Paradise. I was glad I took the time to get to know Chongo and for the lessons I learned from him. The stereotypes surrounding the homeless are that they are drug addicts, mentally ill, or dangerous. Chongo wasn't any of that, nor were the majority of the homeless that would show up on Sundays.

In my personal life, I continued to see Jon in secrecy. We were starting to like each other, but I was being extremely careful. I knew the girls would approve because they already adored him, but I still felt I needed to be cautious and protect their hearts the best I could. I would have him come over when they were asleep, and we would watch a movie or play games, or both do homework. I was back in school finishing my bachelor's degree in psychology. The secrecy went on for about six months. The girls knew I was dating someone, but they didn't know who. When I finally told them who I had been dating, they both laughed hysterically. Yet, they approved. Since I had essentially met him through them, there was not an awkward *meet the kids'* stage. We didn't make our dating public right away, as we didn't know how it would be perceived by others. After all, the after-school teacher was dating the hot mom, and he was nine years younger than me.

Since we were both in college, we would stay up late doing homework often. Since I had my kids so young, I'd missed the traditional college experience and hadn't stayed up late doing college papers with anyone, and I found it pretty fun. We would finish our homework and make a skillet meal with Texas toast at midnight, stay up for a few more hours, and hardly get sleep, but we enjoyed all of it.

I completed my bachelor's in psychology and immediately decided to go for my Ph.D. It was a big decision and something I knew would take a lot of time and dedication. But I wanted to do it for the girls. There are so many stereotypes about single parents, young parents, interracial couples, and interracial children, not to mention stigmas based on income, how far your parents had gone with their education, where you live, and so on.

I never understood many of these stereotypes. I have witnessed many two-parent households that are far more unstable than homes with one loving parent. As a single mother, you feel like people don't expect you to go far in life. You feel people question what kind of role model you can be to your kids, as if you chose to raise them on your own. These assumptions can cause a single mother to feel as if her temporary struggles place a permanent negative value on her self-worth. I was stuck in that terrible way of thinking for years, and when you think that way about yourself, you only attract more pain and hurt. It's a terrible cycle.

Additionally, there are stereotypes that surround the kids who are raised by a single parent. They are deemed troubled, unstable, and bound to fail simply because there is only one parent and not two.

I didn't care what opinions others had of me as much as I cared about the perceptions my daughters would have of themselves. I didn't want them to translate the opinions of others into their reality. I thought a lot about it. What more could I do to be more influential to my daughters, my peers, and the many people who could relate to my journey? That is the thought process that led me to decide to get my PhD. I didn't even know what field to do it in. All I knew is that I wanted to become a doctor, because doctors are valued and respected. They are viewed as smart and competent. People look to doctors for their opinions and help. While I already felt smart and knew I had the potential to influence others in a positive way, I didn't feel valued, or respected. I wanted to feel that too. I was determined to earn my Ph.D. and show my daughters and anyone who would listen, that stereotypes are just opinions.

6 BUILDING RESILIENCE

When Diamond made it to junior high, I wanted to get her into a good school. One of the top schools listed was near downtown, and I wanted her to go there. Since we didn't live near the school, I had to enter Diamond into a lottery system and hope she would get randomly selected if they had openings. We got lucky, and she was chosen. I didn't mind the drive. It was a large school, with over seven hundred kids in the seventh grade alone. This was much larger than her small elementary school, but I wanted her to have the best options.

Diamond was incredibly social and great at making friends. Although, we quickly learned that the school was not as great as we thought it would be, and it didn't have the family feel we were used to at the smaller school. It was also not as diverse as I had thought, being in Midtown. I immediately tried getting involved with the school events as I had before but was snubbed by one of the head parents when she realized I was a single mom and wouldn't be able to help as much financially as the other parents involved. She told me that she could probably find something for me to help with, but they were mainly looking for parents who could help with their fundraising efforts. Could I not help with that? An assumption was made that I couldn't. At the previous school, I'd helped with the bake sales, the carnivals, and getting donations from businesses for prizes! I was too offended and didn't feel I should have to plead my case to another parent, so I let it go.

Before seventh grade, Diamond was in honors classes and doing well. She didn't have to study much and was naturally good at math and English. I had always had a great relationship with the girls' teachers, and when I noticed Diamond was struggling in one of her classes, I reached out to the teacher to set up an appointment. In meetings I'd had with teachers in the past, they would typically go over where the girls had an opportunity to improve and provide suggestions. This time, when I asked about where Diamond could

improve, her only suggestion to me was to hire a tutor.
Well, I couldn't afford that, so I just tried to help her
myself. I quickly learned that math was very different
from how it had been when I learned it, so I was not
much help at all. I reached out to the teacher again to see
if there were any free tutoring options available at the
school, or if she was available anytime during the day to
help the kids, and her response to me was a question:
"Has her father tried to help her at home as well?" I
don't know if that was her indirect way of asking if there
was a father in the home or not, but I reacted
distastefully. I admire and respect teachers, and I
wouldn't normally react that way, but in this case, I felt
she didn't care at all, and I was frustrated. Little did I
know how much my reaction to her would backfire on
me.

Diamond was able to maintain a good C in that
class, but it was clear to me that her teacher had spoken
to the other teachers, as I no longer got a great vibe from
any of them. Despite my continued efforts to be involved
in school activities, I was not "chosen" to help with any
of them the entire year. As the end of the school year
approached, I received a call from CPS while I was at
work. They told me that I needed to meet them at the

school and that an officer had picked up Destiny from her elementary school and would meet me at Diamond's school. Naturally, I was frantic, as they wouldn't share any details with me on the phone, and I didn't know if Diamond was OK or not.

When I got to the school, I was told to sit in an empty classroom. They told me that my daughters were in the next room and that they needed to question me. I didn't understand what was going on. They told me if I didn't cooperate, I could be at risk of losing my kids. I was so worried and stressed that I was struggling to breathe. In the doorway of the classroom, I could see the same teacher that I'd had an issue with speaking to Child Protective Services.

I wish I could relive that moment knowing what I know now about the system... but it was one of those live-and-learn moments.

A social worker pulled me into a smaller area away from everyone and began to question me. She asked if I was aware of any abuse happening to my daughters. My heart sank so far below the surface with terrible thoughts about who could be hurting my girls. If they weren't at school, I was with them. I asked if something had happened to them. I needed to see them. I wanted to know what the hell was going on! She was just staring at me, and I kept asking if something happened and demanded to see them.

She paused, then asked me if I had a learning disability that prevented me from understanding the context of the question. I will never forget how I felt at that moment. I felt like not only was I indirectly being called stupid, but that I had a woman in front of me on a clear power trip. I had to stay calm so I could figure out what was going on. In my mind, I was beating the shit out of her, but understanding what the consequences of my actions would be, I reluctantly kept my cool and replied, "No, I have no learning disabilities, and I am not aware of any abuse happening to my children."

She then shared that during class, one of Diamond's classmates had passed her a note that alluded to a bad home experience. Diamond, trying to relate and be a good friend, had responded to the girl on the note and passed it back sharing that her grandpa (my mom's ex-husband) had kissed her wrong (referring to the fishy kiss incident five years earlier). The girl's mother had found the note in her daughter's backpack and told the teacher. The teacher, instead of asking me about it or telling me about it, immediately called CPS. I don't know if that was standard protocol, but I do know the previous school would never have done that, because they knew the type of mother I was and all that I did for my girls.

I tried to tell the social worker the story and to explain that because of that incident we had not seen him since that night. I told her I had handled it the best that I could have.

Well, she disagreed. She said that she planned to get to the bottom of the situation. She said they were going to interview both of the girls separately in the other room, and I had to sit there for two hours while they did. Words can't express what I went through in those two hours, not because I was afraid of anything they would hear, but because my daughters were having to experience this unnecessary shit and I couldn't be with them.

When she came back into the room she asked about my ex-boyfriend, Calvin, who we also hadn't seen in about five years. She asked me if he had ever spanked the girls. I was honest and said yes. She then brought out a piece of paper. This paper (which I didn't know at the time I didn't have to sign) essentially listed a bunch of things that I had to do in order to keep my kids, or that is how it was put to me.

I signed the papers, got my girls, and got the hell away from that damn school as quickly as possible. When we got home, I asked the girls a hundred times to please tell me if they had ever been abused or if anything had ever happened to them that I didn't know about. I was worried they weren't telling me something. They both confirmed they had not been harmed by anyone and that the people interviewing them had asked them if I had ever had any boyfriends and if the boyfriends had ever spanked them. When asked that question, Diamond was honest and shared that Calvin used to spank them.

After reading the document more closely, I realized that by signing the paper, I was essentially admitting guilt. This document also wanted me to file restraining orders with the court on both Calvin and my mother's ex-husband, even though we had not seen either in five years and we were not at risk, nor did we feel unsafe, and neither of them even knew where we lived. It took all the money I had, and I had to take out a loan for the rest, to hire an attorney.

The attorney started by telling me I shouldn't have signed the document, but because I did, I now had to go file the restraining orders with the court. I went and did that right away, being fully and completely honest, and both restraining orders were denied by the court.

It was a long process. My hair started falling out by the handful: I had never been so stressed in my life. The attorney was working on it and in the meantime, I had to do everything on the stupid document I'd signed, which also included home visits by the same sarcastic social worker I had met at the school. Jon and I had been dating for about a year now, and he was at my home often. I had the social worker meet him at one of the meetings, and she told me she didn't feel I should have another man around my kids. She recommended in her feedback I wait at least two more years. She was treating me like I was this hoe of a mother that just had a bunch of men around my girls. Jon was only my fourth boyfriend if you count my online experience. The girls had only built a relationship with Calvin, and now Jon over five years later. Her snide comments were degrading and often unprofessional and unnecessary. I was so angry that I Googled her, found her Facebook, and had nightmares about this woman who was making my life a living hell when I didn't deserve it.

I understand social workers are needed and help many children who are in bad situations. I once gave up what would have been the biggest listing of my real estate career, valued at just over a million dollars, because I chose to call CPS for a child who was living in terrible conditions. The owner of this once-beautiful property lived in the Bay Area and had not been by to see his home and renters in over two years. When I viewed the home to list it, it was full of transients, people shooting up drugs in the backyard, guns laid out on tables, and maggots all over the kitchen. There was a young boy there around five years old who offered to show me around. He was barefoot and filthy. His bedroom had drug needles on his dresser, and his mattress had no sheets and a huge hole in the middle of it, as if a dog had chewed it up, and had stains all over it. I then noticed the bruises on his arms and legs and felt his conditions were unsafe, so I called CPS, and for my own safety, I let go of that listing. I later found out the boy was reunited with his five siblings who had previously been removed from the home. I am not sure how or why they left him there in those dangerous conditions.

But my kids weren't in any danger at all. I didn't deserve this, nor did they. It was embarrassing, brought up bad memories, and put me in debt. Ultimately, the attorney got CPS off my back. It left me completely broke but sane again. After it was over, I filed a former complaint against the social worker, but nothing was ever done about it, and my many attempts to speak to her supervisor were ignored.

Family

My relationship was going strong, and we found out I was pregnant. It hadn't been planned or expected, and I was on birth control. We both panicked a little, but then we accepted it. We loved each other, but we both wanted to enjoy each other more and would have preferred to have waited.

Summer was approaching, and the girls were taking their traditional Florida trip to see my mom for a couple of weeks. This time I took Jon with me to meet the Florida family and to show him around Orlando. We went to Disney World and a water park with the girls. Disney was fun. Typically, Diamond and Jon would go on the crazy roller coasters, while Destiny and I would go find the closest Dippin' Dots and then meet them at the exit. When we went to the water park, we took my Grandma Hazel's car and parked it near a ravine in the parking lot near many other cars. We had so much fun and stayed until the park closed. When we got back to the car and opened the door, we discovered that large roaches had found their way inside the car. For the entire thirty-minute drive home, the girls and I were sitting frantically in the back seat with our legs up on the seat and the lights on while Jon drove us back to Grandma's house.

When we got back home from Florida, we started to plan for the baby. I wanted to buy my first home, and while I didn't have much money for a down payment, the first-time homebuyer programs were amazing and required hardly anything down. My Realtor found me a great deal on a remodeled four-bedroom that I put an offer on right away. The offer was approved, and I was in escrow on my first home. I was thirty-three at the time.

Meanwhile, we had our appointment to find out the sex of the baby.

During the ultrasound, I could see that the nurse was trying to find the heartbeat. Having had one before, I was worried when I didn't hear that familiar helicopter sound. The nurse excused herself and grabbed the doctor. The doctor then gave it a shot, with no luck. Apparently, the baby's heart had stopped beating at around twelve weeks. We were currently at fifteen and a half weeks. I had to have a procedure to remove the baby, as the miscarriage was not going to happen naturally. It was a sad moment, and a sadness we dealt with for years. We continued with our relationship, and I chose a different type of birth control. We still moved into the four-bedroom when escrow closed, and rather than having a baby room, we made it a man cave.

We decided to take a family trip to Catalina Island to get some positive vibes in our system after all the stress we had all been through. While there, we enjoyed the beach, went in a submarine to look at fish, and rented bikes to ride up to the botanical gardens. Destiny was a little nervous due to the bike accident she'd had in Florida, but she wanted to be brave. We biked all the way up and took some pictures of the scenery, and then it was time to ride back down. The hill was steep, and biking up the hill had been a little strenuous, so going back down the hill, we would need to ride the brakes a little. Jon went first, and I stayed in the back so I could see the girls and they would be between us.

It was like slow motion. I watched as Diamond almost lost control and braked near Destiny. Then I saw Destiny brake abruptly and fly off her bike. I watched as her body rolled a few times before stopping. I started to speed up to get to her. I saw people running to her and couldn't tell how bad it was yet. When I got there, I asked Diamond to ride the rest of the way back down to grab Jon. Destiny was taken to the hospital on the island. Luckily, she had no major injuries, just bruises, and cuts. The next day we all went zip-lining and finished the vacation on a good note. Destiny has not been back on a bike since.

Going on two years of dating, Jon and I were having fun together. One weekend he set up a couple's photo shoot with a photographer who was a friend and asked me to choose a few outfits. During the shoot, when we had our formal outfits on, he asked me to marry him, so that the moment could be captured on camera. Of course, I said yes. I think some people were happy for us, and others couldn't see past me being a little older with kids. I wanted to travel and experience things in life, and he was such a fun person to do them with. Plus, he already had a positive relationship with the girls. To me, it felt like a no-brainer.

Wedding planning was fun. Our goal was to have a big party. We wanted everyone to just have a good time. We decided to get married the day after my birthday and a week after his; that way each year we could celebrate all three events during the same week and do something really fun. For the wedding, we hired a DJ and a bartender. We had an open bar and a photo booth. Both Diamond and Destiny were my maid of honor. Our colors were teal, dark gray, and white. I wasn't picky with the dresses and just told the bridesmaids to pick a teal dress, so that way they would feel comfortable in whatever they chose. I did have many bridesmaids, which included a mix of my childhood friends (Tara, Shannon, and Susan) and my more recent friends I had met through volleyball. During the wedding, we had a sand ceremony to incorporate the girls. We each had our favorite color of sand and added it to a clear keepsake bottle to make a pretty pattern that intertwined to show that the marriage was about all of us. My mom stayed for a week after the wedding to watch the girls at the house while my new husband and I went to Hawaii for our honeymoon.

We went to Kauai. It was absolutely beautiful. We went to a luau, ate far too much, went on a tough hike, and even went skydiving. While skydiving, we had to stuff ourselves into the back of an extremely small aircraft that only fit the two of us and the people that we were attached to on the way down. We sat patiently as the aircraft reached the appropriate height and then jumped out. For a moment we went through a patch of thick clouds. I had my eyes open but couldn't see anything as we were going through the cloud and just felt the moisture of the air. It was a remarkable experience. An adrenaline rush for sure.

When we arrived back home and all our company left, I tried to work on getting the house cozy. I loved decorating it for different holidays, especially Christmas, since it felt warm and happy. Every Easter, Thanksgiving, and Christmas, the girls and I would do something different for the homeless. For Easter, we would make Easter baskets full of essentials such as deodorant, washcloths and soap, water and snacks, toothbrush, and pen and paper to write with. At Thanksgiving, we would participate in the Run to Feed the Hungry, then buy coffee and breakfast after the race and pass it out to the homeless we would find on the streets. For Christmas, we would buy Christmas boxes and pack them full of some essentials and pass those out as well. We introduced Jon to these traditions, and it was nice to have someone else to share those experiences with.

In the meantime, I was still on the hunt for a far

more diverse middle school for the girls to attend. In the role I had as a regional manager, I helped manage a unique property that had apartments on the top with retail spaces below, including a bookstore, Underground Books. I stopped by and was speaking to the owner of the bookstore about my search for a good diverse school, and she told me about two schools down the street that were part of a non-profit run by some great people. It was PS7 Middle School, with Sacramento Charter High School right next to it on the same property. I looked into it and saw the value. The girls would have to wear uniforms, but they would learn great core values. It was mostly African American students who attended this school, and I felt that would also be best for Diamond and Destiny, given they were only ever around my side of the family.

Our house was located across town in a completely different city, and driving them to school every morning took at least an hour (each way), but I did it for five years until Diamond was able to drive: and I would do it again in a heartbeat. It was at least convenient that the schools were located next to each other, so that when Diamond started high school, I could still drop them off at one place and not have to drive to two different locations. We had a high school within walking distance of our house, but I still chose Sacramento Charter High School for them to attend.

Sac High

The girls had grown up around volleyball. Diamond and I would play a game where I wouldn't let her have her M&Ms or any other snack until she could pass the ball to me one hundred times without making a bad pass. Even if we got to ninety-nine, if we missed it, we would start over.

I think it paid off, though, because she made the freshman volleyball team. I couldn't wait to go to the games. I loved going to see the girls play or do anything. Halfway through the freshman volleyball season, the freshman coach had to leave. Diamond volunteered me and said that I could finish coaching the team for the rest of the season. I gained approval from work to start an hour earlier and leave an hour earlier every day during the season so I could hold practice after school. It was my first time coaching, and I found that it was very different from playing, especially with a group of teenage girls. Some practices went smoothly, and other days it would be like all their hormones kicked in at once, and we could have been on a reality TV series with all the drama. Overall, though, I loved it. Not many parents are given the opportunity to coach their kids in high school, and I couldn't pass up on that.

I learned a great deal about time management during that period. I had to juggle parenting, marriage, school, work, and now coaching. It was a lot! Then, when the girls started club volleyball, it took up my weekends also. I only ever missed two games. One was for a work trip I had to go on, and the other was during one of my residencies for school. Even then I had one of the assistant coaches FaceTime me so I could still watch virtually and yell through the screen. I had a schedule that I would follow. I would go to work during the day, then coach after school. Then I would come home, spend time with my husband, and wait until everyone went to bed before I started on my schoolwork. It wouldn't be unusual for me to stay up until 2:00 or 3:00 a.m. and then have to get up at 6:30 a.m. I averaged three to five hours of sleep for years.

I received my master's degree in 2015, right after I turned thirty-five. To obtain it, I had to respond to an actual RFP (request for proposal) that pertained to my field of study, industrial-organizational psychology. I needed to obtain a certain score to get my master's and continue with the program en route to my PhD. For the RFP I responded to, I had to create a summer leadership training program for three different groups: high schoolers, aspiring leaders, and those who were already leaders wanting to improve their skills. They were six weeks each, and I had to design everything from my fees to the breakdown of what would be discussed each hour of each day to the content. I'll never forget the moment when I got the results. I was driving but kept a notification on my phone from the school app that would alert me whenever I got a new message. I was in traffic driving home from the Bay Area and saw the notification. I peeked: I had passed... only by 1 percent, but I still passed. I was crying happy tears all the way home. This meant that I would now receive my master's degree and could continue with the program to try and earn my Ph.D. The ridiculous late nights were starting to feel worth it.

Although I was now married, I still took care of the girls financially, as far as paying for things like club volleyball and school clothes. It was my choice. My reason for marrying my husband was that I loved him and knew he would be a positive role model for the girls. My insecurities made me not want to ask for more than that, and my pride didn't want anyone to think I needed more than that. Part of me felt like it wasn't his responsibility, and I didn't want us to feel like the baggage I had felt we were in the past. I always felt I had to prove I was strong and didn't need any help. There was even a time when I had to carry us financially for six months while he went through the Sheriff's Academy. What was different about him compared to my past relationships was that he still bought the groceries and paid some of the bills, and did what he could during that time, which I appreciated. It didn't make him feel good to live off me, and that was a breath of fresh air. While he was going through the Academy, I made flashcards for him and even started to learn the majority of the penal codes and did everything I could to help him prepare for whatever was next. He ended up getting through the academy and got a job right away as a deputy with the Sacramento County Sheriff's Department.

Secrets

It is hard as a parent to know everything going on in your child's life. I know I was able to keep many things from my parents and got away with far more than I likely should have. Because of the mindset I had as a kid, I feel I was able to pick up on a lot of what the girls were going through. I didn't always know the details, but my intuition would kick in enough for me to know if they needed to talk or if something was not right.

They would have their boy crushes here and there but nothing too serious, until Diamond met a guy in high school. I always tried to be open to who the girls liked, because I remembered what it was like for me, and I didn't want them to feel that way. Instead, I wanted them to feel supported and to know they could talk to me if they needed to. Well, I didn't have good vibes about this guy at all, but Diamond liked him, so I kept trying to like him too. What I didn't like was the way Diamond changed. She was typically bubbly, outgoing, and silly... but with this guy, I felt she suddenly had low confidence and was quiet and a tad distant. It wasn't like her at all. Having been there to know the sorts of things a person can do or say to you to make you feel that way, I was worried about her.

As a mother or just a parent in general, you have to be cautious about how you approach certain situations. If your kids fail to do their chores or their homework, that's one thing... you ground them or take their phone for a bit. But when it is something that can affect who they are as a person, you know from experience that how you react as a parent can make a difference. It's tough. I knew something wasn't right with Diamond, and I knew he had something to do with it, but I didn't know how. When I tried to talk to her about it, she wouldn't want me to think negatively of him. She would only tell me how good he was and not say anything bad… just like I did with my parents. This continued for a bit, and then she let me know that they had been arguing.

I felt like it had gotten to the point where she was ready to leave him, but then his stepdad got shot right in front of their house. Of course, she felt obligated to be there for him. Luckily, his stepdad didn't die, but their relationship still wasn't healthy. I noticed at volleyball practice that she had started wearing wristbands or long-sleeved shirts even when it was hot outside. She was cutting herself and trying to hide it. As soon as I saw this, I confronted her about it. She assured me that everything was fine and that she wouldn't do it again. She said that it was more because other girls were doing it and she had wanted to see how it felt. She was so stressed, and my heart was breaking for her, not knowing how to help other than talk to her as much as I could.

Being there every day to coach during volleyball season helped me stay in tune with things, but I still didn't know everything going on. The basketball team often had practice right after our volleyball practice. One day one of their star players started coming early and would ask if she could use one of the hoops in the corner while we were still in our practice. I allowed her to, as I appreciated her work ethic. She and Diamond became friends pretty quickly. Before I knew it, Diamond was starting to act herself again. She broke up with her boyfriend and started hanging out with her new friend regularly. She was bubbly again and getting her confidence and her silly personality back, and my heart was happy.

Eventually, I found out they were actually in a relationship. The other girl was a grade higher than Diamond. To my knowledge, Diamond hadn't liked girls in the past, so I hadn't thought anything of it, but once I found out, it did make sense. Shit, I didn't care at all. I was just relieved that I didn't have to worry about her mental health and was happy that she was happy. To see her coming back to herself was all I cared about. It wasn't as easy for my husband to swallow, as he had been raised in a heavily Christian household and felt same-sex relationships just weren't right. Eventually, he came around and was supportive of their relationship. Diamond and her girlfriend went to prom together and both looked beautiful in their dresses. The stereotypes that all gay girls are "not lady-like," or that one must be "the boy" are simply not true. Go figure.

I know my daughters had a part of them that wished they were going to a bigger high school where they didn't have to wear uniforms, but choosing that school was a decision I would have made over and over again. It was worth all the miles and all the hours of driving. I would get asked all the time why I didn't just have them go to the school around the corner. While that school would have given them a high school diploma, it would not have taught them as much about their Black culture, which was knowledge I lacked. I probably wouldn't have ended up coaching them, and the hour-long drives led to some of the best conversations with them, which I will always cherish. Sometimes we would all be too tired to talk during the commute, so I would put on some Lauryn Hill or India Arie, and we would all just sing instead. Had I chosen to make it easier on myself and just had them walk to the nearby school… I would have missed all those special moments.

7 NO STOP SIGNS

It's weird when your kids turn eighteen and they are considered an adult by law, but you know damn well they aren't REALLY. You begin to watch them make decisions you know may not be the best, but they are an adult now and you want them to live and learn, so you do your best to guide them and hope that all you taught them was enough.

For anyone who has an assumption that parenting stops at eighteen, let me assure you, it is a highly mistaken idea. I would even say that it is when your kids need you the most. It's a scary time for them, trying to figure out what they want to do, how they're going to do it, and knowing there will be lots of trial and error. It was important to me that they knew I would be there along the way.

For Diamond's eighteenth birthday, we went on a cruise to Mexico. We ported out of Long Beach and cruised to Catalina Island and Ensenada. It was the first time the girls had been able to use their passports, and they had a good time. It was crazy for me to think that I had given birth to Diamond when I was her age.

Diamond went and got her first tattoo for her birthday. It was a small flower behind her ear. I hadn't gotten any tattoos yet, but I wasn't against it either. It was her body, and while as a mother I hoped she wouldn't get anything crazy; I know for her it was self-expression. Jon wasn't crazy about it, but in time he became more open to it and even eventually got one of his own.

Diamond wasn't certain what direction she wanted to go in, career-wise, so she decided to play volleyball at a junior college about forty-five minutes away. I was ecstatic that she was staying reasonably close, and my pockets were ecstatic I didn't have to try to figure out four-year college tuition. I felt bad that Diamond didn't qualify for financial aid because they combined my income with my husband's. Even though he didn't pay or have any obligation to pay for any of their schooling or activities, they wouldn't just use my income alone. The classes were not that expensive, but the books! That is one of the biggest rip-offs in our country, in my opinion. I had to put several books on credit cards because I didn't have the cash, and when you are finished with the books and the class, even if you paid $300 for the book, you are not able to sell it for even half of that, because by the following year a new book would be needed for that class, and the one you purchased for your kid was now worthless.

Diamond moved out with a teammate of hers, and I was happy for her to experience living on her own, though I was still sobbing when she left. As a parent, you want to be able to protect them and keep them safe at all times. She moved from that apartment to her best friend's house after a few months, as they had an extra room and it was much cheaper.

I drove to all of Diamond's home games that I was able to make and a few of her away games; I loved watching her play in college. We developed a routine. After the games, we would grab tacos at a popular spot in town and talk about the game, and then I would drive back home.

Destiny was in her senior year of high school, and

we were busy doing all the senior year activities. We ordered her prom dress online: when it came in the mail just before prom, it looked very different from the photo. It was a couple hundred dollars, and we couldn't return it. I could tell that Destiny was trying to make it work for my sake because she knew we would be down on the money if we couldn't, but I could also tell by her face that she absolutely hated it. Quite frankly, I did too. The photo was of this beautiful red, long-sleeved gown that had an open back and lace on the sleeves, with intricate laced weaving throughout. What we received looked like something a grandmother would wear to a funeral, made with cheap material, and the open back had a nylon mesh that was at least three shades lighter than Destiny's skin tone. It was really bad. Prom was about two weeks away, and now we had to find a replacement dress. We searched everywhere and finally found a beautiful royal-blue-and-gold dress she looked stunning in.

She was playing her last year of club volleyball and trying to figure out what college to go to. She missed her sister and changed her volleyball number to her sister's number for her senior year. California passed a new law that would allow California residents to attend their first two years of junior college for free! Of course, we took advantage of this. She wanted to attend the junior college that was closest to our house, as she had recently gotten her first car and didn't like driving yet. She wanted to play volleyball in college, but the college she had signed up for already had two setters returning and one new setter they'd picked up. Diamond's team needed a setter. I was selfishly trying to persuade Destiny to play on Diamond's team so I could see them play together again, but she didn't want that commute, and I understood. She signed up for her classes at the junior college nearby and got more hours at work since she no longer had volleyball. Coincidentally, Destiny's first job was at Champs in the mall.

I found a way to keep us all playing volleyball together. I signed us up to play on a team together at the same place I used to take them when they were little, when I was earning extra money refereeing. It was the three of us and one of Diamond's teammates on a team, and we would play and compete once a week four-on-four. Our team name was Volleymambas. Mamba being from Kobe Bryant, of course.

As adults, the girls are so alike and yet so different. Diamond likes to learn from trial and error. People love her the moment they meet her and want to be around her energy. She is a fantastic writer and is creative with her self-expression and writes poems. You can't tell her much; she needs to experience things for herself. She likes to take risks and try new things. I was the same way when I was her age, and I try to remember that and acknowledge that I am still alive and doing all right. However, she is far brighter than I was at her age, so I know she will be all right too.

Destiny is more of an observer and likes things she is comfortable with. She likes the comfort of her own bed. She doesn't trust many people and will keep you at arm's length until she does, but if you do happen to break through her walls, she is a great, loyal friend to have. She can play the piano by ear and can write and sing a thoughtful song that would make you cry in about ten minutes. She can draw and designs her own artwork, which she hangs in her room.

They both have the biggest hearts and don't judge people based on their circumstances. They are beautiful and kind, and I'm so grateful they have each other.

8 WHAT'S UP, DOC?

I wanted to finish my Ph.D. before the girls finished high school, but when you start the process, you don't realize it can often take much longer than the planned schedule shows. The girls knew I was working on it the whole time. I never took time off from school. There were certain parts I had to wait on, which gave me a break here and there, but that didn't happen often.

At my first residency, I remember seeing people who were in their fifth and sixth year of the program, just the doctoral part after they obtained their master's. I remember judging them because I wondered why someone would spend so much damn money and take their time on this. Eventually, I realized how it could take a person several years to finish. It is not cheap or easy. I also understood why many people do not work while they go through this process. It is extremely stressful and mentally draining, and it requires an enormous amount of discipline and commitment.

The handful of doctors we were able to meet and learn from at the residencies were fantastic, and best of all, I got to see my classmates in person. One in particular, Leslye, I became good friends with. Having a friend to go through the process with who you can vent to outside of the classroom is a necessity. Over and over again, we leaned on each other and pushed ourselves to the next level. One day in class at one of the residencies, I quoted Tupac in the classroom, "Through all the rain and the pain, you gotta keep your sense of humor. You gotta smile through all the bullshit." Our older White professor had no idea who I was talking about. She had never heard of Tupac! So... I gave her a homework assignment (with the assistance of a few of my classmates) that she had to listen to Tupac's "Changes," "Keep Ya Head Up," and "Dear Mama" and share her thoughts with us the next day. Meanwhile, as a class, we were assigned different theorists to present on.

The next day came, and not only had she listened to our recommendations, but she had also learned about him, his life, his death, and what an incredible poet he was. She was intrigued and found him talented. I told her that some of his music had gotten me through some of the hardest times in my life. I learned from that experience with her. There was something powerful about sharing perspectives with someone open to learning about something they otherwise may have never known. Regardless if she had heard any stereotypes about rappers or not, she was open to learning and was genuinely curious, and it showed. There was simply no judgment.

I chose to do my dissertation on smartphones and work-life balance. To make it more difficult, I chose to incorporate both quantitative and qualitative data. It ended up being an explanatory sequential mixed-methods study. Writing a dissertation is like writing an obnoxious, repetitive book full of facts and research that support a study: your study. The research, data collection, and data analyses take time and need to be observed, acknowledged, and approved by your chosen dissertation committee with each step. When conducting research on human subjects, before you can even start collecting data, your research plan must be thoroughly written and explained, and sent to the Institutional

Review Board for approval. That process alone took seven months.

I dedicated my dissertation to the girls. It read:

You are the reason I began this journey and my motivation throughout the process. My purpose in pursuing my PhD was to show you that stereotypes can be wrong, and with hard work and discipline, you can achieve anything you put your mind to. I have learned that you are the only thing affecting your situation, and you are the only one who can change it, if you desire to. Thank you for helping our family change for the better and for inspiring me to beat the odds.

When I told people that I was getting my degree in a mostly online environment, I would feel judged for that at times. You know, it's funny—when I was looking into colleges where I would have the opportunity to get a PhD online, there were only two solid, accredited options that I knew of at the time. Now almost every college offers it, but it is still frowned upon by some. For me, online was my only option, and I was grateful to have the opportunity to earn my degree. I will share from experience the observation that, while it may be possible for a person to earn a bachelor's degree for another person online, it would be very difficult to do the same for a master's and a PhD. The residencies are in-person, and if you are not the person doing the work and you don't understand the material, you won't pass. My school had a 30-percent PhD completion rate. It took me seven years total: three years to earn my master's and then an additional four years to earn my PhD, with no breaks. The stereotypes that indicate online schooling is a way of paying for your degree to get it quickly, and that it is much easier, are simply not true.

Don't get me wrong: I would have loved to have gone to Long Beach State and not worked while my parents paid for everything. But I am grateful for my experience, and now that I have gone through it, I would rather hire a person who worked full-time, raised two kids, coached high school volleyball, and earned their PhD over someone who just got the degree from the brick-and-mortar without the life experience. But that's just me. Perhaps I am a little biased.

I remember when it was time to defend my study. This happens when your research is complete, it is approved by everyone, and all your credits are finished, but now you need to prove yourself and what you have learned, or else you don't pass. You must defend your study and show how your new research is relevant and useful to the field. I am not able to discuss the details of the defense, but it is essentially a panel interview where they take turns asking you several questions to ensure they feel confident releasing you into the world as a "doctor." When the defense was over, I had to wait while they deliberated. My dissertation chair then said to me, "Congratulations, Dr. Candice."

It was done.

We did it. We broke a stereotype. My daughters will forever know that stereotypes are nothing but opinions and that we have a choice in everything. We can always choose our path. That was my goal and my only goal in getting my PhD. It was important to me to set an example as their parent and show them that obstacles don't define you. There is always a way to get through it. But you have to want it, and you have to put in the work.

Granted, what I owe in student loan debt is more than what most people owe on their mortgage, but it was worth it. I would do it all over again if it meant knowing my daughters would feel stronger and more confident because of it.

So was it true? Did people respect me more and

think I was smarter after I earned my PhD?

Yeah, they did. I have mixed feelings about that.

To celebrate, Jon and I took the girls to New Orleans, where my childhood friend Susan now lived, and my other childhood friend Shannon flew and met us there. I had been there before with Shannon for Susan's wedding, and I knew Jon and the girls would love the atmosphere there. Diamond, Destiny, and I got matching ankle tattoos of a lotus flower, which symbolizes an unbreakable bond. I never imagined I would get tattoos with my kids, but I highly recommend it.

I was looking forward to graduation and couldn't wait for my family to see me get my degree. A couple weeks beforehand, I was sitting at the airport in Phoenix with two of my co-workers when I received a text message from my brother in Oregon asking if Dad was OK. I had just taken him to breakfast a few days earlier, so I assumed he was fine. My brother told me he had received a message from my dad saying that he thought he might have broken his hip. I tried calling, but he wasn't answering the phone. He called me back sounding like he was completely out of breath. He told me he had fallen and hurt himself two nights earlier but hadn't wanted to bother me with it. He said he couldn't walk. I called Jon, who had just gotten off duty, and asked if he could please stop by and check on Dad to see how bad it was.

He called me about twenty minutes later, just as I was boarding the plane, to tell me it looked like a murder scene. There was blood everywhere. My father had tripped and fallen just perfectly on a wooden table tray and managed to shatter his hip bone. Then he had continued to try and walk on it and had fallen eleven more times, with one being a headfirst fall into the toilet, which had given him a head wound that had knocked him out. The blood all over the floor was from carpet burn on his opposite knee from him dragging himself around the apartment. He lived in an upstairs unit, and Jon didn't want to hurt him more by trying to carry him, so he called an ambulance. The ambulance came, and I requested they take him to UC Davis Medical Center. It wasn't that he hadn't wanted to bother me, it was that he didn't want me to be disappointed in him. Even in the greatest pain of his life, he was worried about my feelings. Alcoholism is a terrible disease. I don't know when the relapse began this time, but he hid it well until he binged.

There was a poem that my dad wrote while he was

in rehab the last time about his addiction. This poem creatively reflects his perspective when dealing with the disease. With his permission, I share it with you.

To My Best Bud,

Buddy, we've known each other for a long time… 40 years, since high school. No matter where I moved, you always kept in contact with me. One of the things about you… you always bring friends. Seldom do you travel alone. I've seen you bring 5 or 35 (friends).

We've had some great times… the parties, BBQs, and picnics. Most of the time, lately… it's just me, you, and your "friends" hanging out at the house.

Whether I have felt lonely and sad, or angry, you always seemed to calm me down… although, you would usually need to come back the next day. That ice-cold attitude of yours is really something.

One of the things that started bothering me lately is that you make me nervous. Sometimes, I shake so bad, I can't hold a glass of water. You know how I feel about cheese… I despise it. Well, you're starting to smell like cheese.

Anyway, Bud, I've decided to get out more, do a little traveling… see the sights. And in doing this, I just can't have you around anymore.

*If you feel it necessary to knock on my door again, don't
bother. I'm moving on and you're not getting my new
address.*

*I'll probably see you from time to time in other places,
but pardon me if I don't say hi.*

PKB

When the plane landed, I went straight to the
hospital. The surgeons were straightforward with me and
told me they needed to operate right away because his
leg was black from the hip to the knee and he was
bleeding too much internally; however, they couldn't
operate right away because he was in the middle of
detoxing, and his sodium level was too low to put him
under. They pumped him full of many things trying to
raise his salt level, and he was not able to eat. He was
hallucinating and was continuously ripping the catheter
out from down below. It was like this for almost two
days, and then the surgeon came and spoke to me again.
He said they needed to wait longer but they couldn't,
and they weren't going to, because they wanted to try
and save not only his leg but also his life. They told me
that there was a good chance he might not wake up after
they put him under and shared with me that my father
had a do-not-resuscitate order. They told me they wanted

me to understand that and that they would try their best. They estimated the surgery would take about three to four hours.

I waited for five and a half hours. I had chosen to be by myself, because I felt the surgeon was trying to prepare me for the worst and I didn't want my girls or anyone else having to experience that initial pain should they tell me that he hadn't made it. When I saw the two surgeons walk into the waiting room, my heart started pounding out of my chest. They asked me to please sit down. The lead surgeon told me that he had been replacing hips for many years and this was by far the worst case he had ever seen. He said it was so horrible they'd had the medical students enter the room during the surgery to witness it, as they would probably never see anything like it again. He said that all the muscle had worn from the bone and there had been nothing to attach a new titanium hip to. They had to place a foreign substance in the leg that hopefully the bone would attach to, and then the plan would be to wait and see if muscle grew and if his body would accept or reject the new foreign object and hip. He did wake up after the surgery, and we knew recovery, if possible, would be a long road.

While my dad was in the hospital, I moved

everything out of his upstairs apartment and into my home. I sold his truck for him, since he wouldn't be driving, and got rid of what wouldn't fit in my place that didn't mean anything to him.

He spent about two weeks in the hospital, just over a month inside a live-in rehabilitation center, and then came to live with us. Destiny and I ended up moving him across the country to Florida to live with my mother as a roommate and companion. He has aches from time to time, but he is walking and is completely self-sufficient now.

He missed my graduation, but he lived... so, no complaints.

Looking Forward

For so long I defined myself through labels society and stereotypes had imposed on me. My parents were divorced; therefore, I came from a broken home. I had two kids by the time I was twenty, and out of wedlock, which made me a slut that was going straight to hell (if you are religious). It was ridiculous. Sure, my parents divorced, but I will tell you, the home was far more "broken" when they were still married than it was after they divorced! After being married for about twenty years and divorced for about twenty years, they became roommates again for companionship. And I turned out OK too. Don't ever feel ashamed about being who you are.

You are who you are.

I am grateful I didn't grow up in a bubble, sheltered from the realities of life, and that I have both street smarts and book smarts. I took what I learned from my parents and applied it to my future choices. I slowly began to understand that I had complete control of my life and its potential. I owned up to my mistakes but did my best to only punish myself once for it, as I learned that dwelling on the past never helped me reach my goals any faster.

Part of me always felt like an underdog. The good part about that is that it gave me a strong urge to succeed. You see, feeling like an underdog is different from feeling like a victim or having a victim mentality. The difference is the way you frame your story and how you understand yourself through that story, not the facts of your life. We are not victims at all; we are leaders with experiences that have equipped us to better lead and succeed.

I'll give you an example. I'll share facts about myself that are all true but framed differently, first from a negative perspective, then from a positive one.

1. I only completed three years of high school.
2. I had two kids by the time I was twenty.
3. I didn't complete my education until I was thirty-nine.

OR

1. I graduated a year early from high school.
2. I have two kids in college.
3. I earned my PhD in industrial-organizational psychology.

All these facts are true, but which perspective should I focus on? No one has a perfect life. So why do we judge people as if they should?

I see the same question in many articles and books on leadership and self-growth: "How do you make the whole better than the sum of its parts?" You just appreciate the parts. Each part plays a role in what the sum turns out to be. Respect and appreciate the journey—your journey. All of it, the good and the bad. I can't honestly say that I would want to experience a lot of what I went through over again, but I know that because I had those experiences, I became wiser, more intuitive, more resilient, and more emotionally intelligent. Those are qualities that some of the best leaders have, so I embrace them.

I once read that in the Navy, they have a 40-percent rule: when you think you are done, you are really only 40-percent done. The more you tap in, the more resilient you become. The strength of being a single mother feels similar. In those times when I didn't think I could do anymore or take anymore, those were the times my love for the girls took over. A single mother's strength is a strength like no other and should be seen as such. Not a burden, not a pity party. A single mother is a soldier fighting to gain the social acceptance she so deserves.

A single father is looked at with awe and respect, because men are groomed to be brave. He is commended for taking care of his responsibilities and applauded for having his priorities in order. It's viewed as sexy.

A single mother feels the pressure, because she is expected to show she can do it all to gain the same acceptance and respect, because women are groomed to be perfect; otherwise, she is viewed as a woman with a bunch of baggage who doesn't have her shit together.

We need equality in the way that single parents are viewed.

Unfortunately, I went through a divorce and wrote this book as a single mother once more. Filing for divorce was hard for me. I am not a quitter, and I fight for the people I love, and it was tough. In looking at the positive, I am grateful I had someone to share major milestones and experiences in our lives with. Many people do not get to experience love at all, and I was blessed to have had it for almost a decade.

After healing from the divorce, I started to love and invest in myself for the first time in my life. It didn't matter as much who did or didn't love me. What mattered was that my character was not broken, my integrity was still intact, my heart was still full, and my daughters had seen me get through it. The process may not have been perfect, but we learn the most from the process, and so I am even grateful for that.

My new lifelong goal is to just continue to inspire those around me in a positive way. I want to give confidence to those who need it. I want to provide hope and motivation to those who need to hear it. And I want to be the example for anyone doubting or second-guessing their potential.

Diamond is now a certified personal trainer and is taking classes to become a nutritionist, and Destiny is finishing a dental program. I could not be prouder of who they are, and I look forward to observing what more they will become. Whatever they decide, it will be with confidence, because they now have no doubt, they can do whatever they put their minds to. I mean, they are the daughters of a doctor... or a single mother... however you choose to look at it.

#MOMDAD

ABOUT THE AUTHOR

Dr. Candice Burney earned her Ph.D. in Industrial-Organizational Psychology; focusing on applying research to increasing workplace productivity, employee engagement, work-life balance, emotional intelligence, and helping with organizational growth. She became a young single mother with two kids by the time she was twenty and faced hardships and stereotypes she was determined to overcome. She now finds passion in elevating others by helping them to realize their true potential. Not the potential society places upon them, but the potential they know to be true within themselves.

Made in the USA
Coppell, TX
31 March 2021